Decolonising Knowledge and Knowers

Decolonising Knowledge and Knowers contributes to the current struggles for decolonising education in the global South, focusing on the highly illuminating case of South African higher education. Galvanised by #FeesMustFall and #RhodesMustFall student protests, South Africa has seen particularly intense and broad social engagement with debates over decolonising universities. However, much of this debate has been consumed with definitions and meanings. In contrast, *Decolonising Knowledge and Knowers* shows how conceptual tools, specifically from Legitimation Code Theory, can be enacted in research and teaching to meaningfully work towards productive decolonisation. Each chapter addresses a key issue in contemporary debates in South African higher education and shows how practices concerning knowledge and knowers are playing a role, drawing on quantitative and qualitative research, praxis, and interdisciplinary research.

Mlamuli Nkosingphile Hlatshwayo is a senior lecturer in Curriculum Studies at the University of KwaZulu-Natal, South Africa. His research interests include theorising transformation in the global South, decolonisation, student movements and epistemological access in curricula.

Hanelie Adendorff is a senior advisor in the Centre for Teaching and Learning at Stellenbosch University, South Africa. She has a PhD in Chemistry but has been working in professional development since 2002.

Margaret A.L. Blackie is a senior lecturer in the Department of Chemistry and Polymer Science at Stellenbosch University, South Africa. Since starting her independent career she has attempted to hold together research interests in both synthetic organic chemistry and education research.

Aslam Fataar is currently Research and Development Professor in Transformation at Stellenbosch University, South Africa. His expertise includes sociology of education and education policy. He has been awarded several medals of honour for contributions to South African education and prizes for his publications.

Paul Maluleka is a South African scholar and Lecturer in History of Education and History Education at the School of Education, University of the Witwatersrand, Johannesburg – South Africa. His interests centre around themes of education decolonisation, de/coloniality, and Africanisation in the South African academe and basic education.

Legitimation Code Theory
Knowledge-building in research and practice
Series editor: Karl Maton
LCT Centre for Knowledge-Building

This series focuses on Legitimation Code Theory or 'LCT', a cutting-edge approach adopted by scholars and educators to understand and improve their practice. LCT reveals the otherwise hidden principles embodied by knowledge practices, their different forms and their effects. By making these 'legitimation codes' visible to be learned or changed, LCT work makes a real difference, from supporting social justice in education to improving design processes. Books in this series explore topics across the institutional and disciplinary maps of education, as well as other social fields, such as politics and law.

Other volumes in this series include:

Teaching Science
Knowledge, Language, Pedagogy
Edited by Karl Maton, J. R. Martin and Y. J. Doran

Decolonising Knowledge and Knowers
Struggles for university transformation in South Africa
Edited by Mlamuli Nkosingphile Hlatshwayo, Hanelie Adendorff,
Margaret A.L. Blackie, Aslam Fataar and Paul Maluleka

Enhancing Science Education
Exploring knowledge practices with Legitimation Code Theory
Edited by Margaret A. L. Blackie, Hanelie Adendorff and Marnel Mouton

Sociology of Possibility
An Invitation to Legitimation Code Theory
Karl Maton

For a full list of titles in this series, please visit: www.routledge.com/Legiti mation-Code-Theory/book-series/LMCT

Decolonising Knowledge and Knowers

Struggles for University Transformation in South Africa

Edited by Mlamuli Nkosingphile Hlatshwayo, Hanelie Adendorff, Margaret A.L. Blackie, Aslam Fataar, and Paul Maluleka

Routledge
Taylor & Francis Group
LONDON AND NEW YORK

First published 2022
by Routledge
4 Park Square, Milton Park, Abingdon, Oxon OX14 4RN

and by Routledge
605 Third Avenue, New York, NY 10158

Routledge is an imprint of the Taylor & Francis Group, an informa business

British Library Cataloguing-in-Publication Data
A catalogue record for this book is available from the British Library

Library of Congress Cataloging-in-Publication Data
Names: Hlatshwayo, Mlamuli Nkosingphile, editor. | Adendorff, Hanelie, editor. |
    Blackie, Margaret A. L., editor. | Fataar, Aslam, editor. | Maluleka, Paul, editor.
Title: Decolonising knowledge and knowers : struggles for university transformation
    in South Africa / edited by Mlamuli Nkosingphile Hlatshwayo, Hanelie
    Adendorff, Margaret A.L. Blackie, Aslam Fataar and Paul Maluleka.
Description: First Edition. | New York : Routledge, 2022. | Series: Legitimation Code
    Theory | Includes bibliographical references and index. | Contents: Introducing
    "decolonizing knowledge and knowers" — Pursuing decolonial knowledge
    building in South African higher education — Building a 'decolonial knower':
    Contestations in the humanities — Decolonising the university: Some thoughts on
    recontextualising knowledge — Towards a decolonized school history curriculum
    in post-apartheid South Africa through enacting Legitimation Code
    Theory — Decolonization and science education: What is at stake? — A decolonial
    science education: How do we move forward?
Identifiers: LCCN 2021060004 | ISBN 9780367618827 (Hardback) |
    ISBN 9780367618841 (Paperback) | ISBN 9781003106968 (eBook)
Subjects: LCSH: Education, Higher—Aims and objectives—South Africa. |
    Educational sociology—South Africa. | Knowledge, Theory of.
Classification: LCC LA1538 .D43 2022 | DDC 378.68—dc23/eng/20220217
LC record available at https://lccn.loc.gov/2021060004

ISBN: 978-0-367-61882-7 (hbk)
ISBN: 978-0-367-61884-1 (pbk)
ISBN: 978-1-003-10696-8 (ebk)

DOI: 10.4324/9781003106968

Typeset in Times New Roman
by Apex CoVantage, LLC

Contents

Figures

Tables

Contributors

Hanelie Adendorff is a senior advisor in the CTL at Stellenbosch University, South Africa. She has a PhD in Chemistry but has been working in professional development since 2002. Her career and professional development started with an interest in blended learning and has since included the areas of assessment, facilitation of collaborative learning, science education, and, more recently, decolonisation of the science curriculum. As a member of the Faculty of Science's teaching and learning hub, she works with the Vice-Dean (Teaching and Learning) to enhance the status of teaching in the Faculty.

Margaret A. L. Blackie is a senior lecturer in the Department of Chemistry and Polymer Science at Stellenbosch University, South Africa. Since starting her independent career she has attempted to hold together research interests in synthetic organic chemistry and in education research. She is passionate about understanding how knowledge in chemistry is built in the field and in the minds of students. She has been the recipient of several awards including the South African Chemical Institute Chemistry Education Medal and the Stellenbosch University Distinguished Teacher Award. She is also recipient of the Stellenbosch University Teaching Fellowship focusing on creating resources to smooth the path for academics from the natural sciences to engage with education research.

Aslam Fataar is a distinguished professor whose scholarship resides in the areas of Sociology of Education and Education Policy. Prof. Fataar is also former Vice Dean, Research of Stellenbosch University's Education Faculty and former Head of the Department of Education Policy Studies. He is currently attached to SU's transformation office in the capacity of Research and Development Professor. He was awarded a medal of honour by the Education Association of South Africa in 2015 for his scholarly and academic development work. Aslam Fataar has been recognised for his outstanding service to the academic study of education, as well as his service in this sector. He was awarded a Medal of Honour by the Education Association of South Africa (EASA), an inclusive organisation of academics, researchers, and practitioners who all prioritise educational research, particularly in South Africa. Aslam has won prizes for three of his published articles. He authored three books, co-authored one, and edited and co-edited six books. He has published over 100 articles and book chapters. He was the previous president of the South African Education Research Association and the Chief Editor of the journal, *Southern African Review of Education*.

Mlamuli Nkosingphile Hlatshwayo is a scholar in the field of Higher Education and Politics. His research interests include theorising transformation in the global South, student movements, issues around epistemological access and curricula, and the philosophy of education. He has an established research publication record in the transformation of the South African education system. Currently, he is a Senior Lecturer in the discipline of Curriculum Studies at the School of Education, University of KwaZulu-Natal. He supervises postgraduate students and teaches both undergraduate and postgraduate courses to education students in the B.Ed and M.ED programmes. He holds a PhD in Higher Education Studies and a master's degree (Cum Laude) in Political and International Studies from Rhodes University. Dr Hlatshwayo is a well-known public intellectual, who commentates in the media on the state of education and politics in South Africa. Dr Hlatshwayo currently serves as the editorial board member for *Critical Studies in Teaching and Learning* (CriSTal), and the *Journal of Educational Studies* (JES). He is currently serving nationally as the project manager in the Higher Education Learning and Teaching Association of Southern Africa's (HELTASA) National Interest Group on Decolonisation.

Kathy Luckett is Emeritus Professor in the Centre for Higher Education Development and currently works for the Institutional Planning Department, University of Cape Town. She teaches and supervises on the School of Education's Masters in Higher Education Studies and in the Department of Sociology. Her research interests are higher education policy around equity, access, and language; sociology of knowledge; and curriculum studies with a focus on the humanities, Africana, decolonial and post-colonial studies, and research methods that apply social realism to educational evaluation.

Paul Maluleka is a South African scholar and Lecturer in History of Education and History Education at the School of Education, University of the Witwatersrand (Wits), Johannesburg – South Africa. He was once a teaching assistant (Assistant Lecturer) of History Education, as well as a Member of the Executive Committee – the highest decision making body of the school – as a Graduate Student Representative at the same institution. Maluleka also lectured at the University of Limpopo's School of Education. Maluleka's research and teaching interests centre around themes of education decolonisation, de/coloniality, and Africanisation in the South African academe and basic education. Maluleka holds a Master of Education (by research) in History Education with distinction from Wits. He is currently reading for his DPhil Education (PhD) with Wits, and is also a doctoral fellow at the National Institute for the Humanities and Social Sciences.

Neo Lekgotla *laga* Ramoupi is South African and Senior Lecturer: History in the School of Education at Wits University, Johannesburg, where he's the Chairperson of the Transformation Committee of the School. He received his PhD from Howard University, Washington D.C., USA (2013); where he was a researcher at SARAP (2004–2006). He was a researcher in the Heritage & Resources Department at Robben Island Museum from 2000 to 2003. When he returned from the USA, he was employed by the Nelson Mandela Foundation (NMF) from 2006 to 2007. He is the co-editor of a recent book, *Robben Island Rainbow Dreams: The making of democratic South Africa's first National Heritage Institution* (2021). Dr Ramoupi is also Advisory Board Member of America's Voices Against Apartheid (AVAA).

1 Introducing 'decolonising knowledge and knowers'

Mlamuli Nkosingphile Hlatshwayo,
Hanelie Adendorff, Margaret A.L. Blackie,
Aslam Fataar, and Paul Maluleka

Universities in the global South and beyond are engaged in protracted struggles for higher education transformation and decolonisation (Mbembe, 2016; Ndlovu-Gatsheni, 2013). The purpose of the university, its epistemic foundations, curricula, and assessment practices have been at the receiving end of decolonial critique. These debates have been taking place in South Africa, the United Kingdom, the United States, Aotearoa New Zealand, Australia, Turkey, India, Latin America, and Caribbean countries. At the heart of all these struggles is the challenge of how to decolonise higher education beyond the emotive and simplistic binary discourses that have hitherto characterised such critical conversations. With its history of settler colonialism and apartheid, South Africa offers a deeply insightful case study for exploring these debates more closely. This book focuses on the decolonisation of education in South Africa, with a specific emphasis on curriculum knowledge.

The 2015–2016 student movements sparked the call for decolonisation in South African higher education. This call included decentring Western epistemologies in higher education curriculum, troubling the alienating nature of university curricula, and the need to transform teaching and learning practices. The imperative to decolonise education has become a constitutive feature of the politics of knowledge at universities.

This book addresses two concerns that persist in current decolonisation debates. The first is a concern about the fractious and emotive tone that recontextualisation decolonisation debates. Some students and scholars have posited these debates as an either/or dichotomy, calling us to think beyond the discourses of 'dead white men' in our educational practices. The second concern is the need to foreground how decolonial debates tend to collapse ontological and epistemological considerations when proposing various ways of achieving decolonial aims. We believe that focusing on these two aims will allow for a more rigorous engagement to integrate decolonisation into education and curriculum policy and practice. The

DOI: 10.4324/9781003106968-1

South African context provides a particular perspective because the debates and protests in this country have pushed decolonisation onto the national agenda. We argue that what is required is an approach that can advance the decolonial debate and propose some necessary curriculum, teaching, and learning interventions.

This book brings together a multidisciplinary group of South African scholars who present a decolonising education approach that places knowledge-building at the heart of the sociology of education. This book contributes to calls for *re*centring Africa-centred knowledge forms in curriculum knowledge-building. We support the view that despite 'the normativising effect of colonialism on marginalising African knowledge, [such knowledge forms] remain alive on the continent and [are] currently reproduced in various forms' (Fataar and Subreenduth, 2015, p. 107). The book addresses the marginalisation of African knowledge in formalised settings such as the university and its curriculum. We critique the workings of epistemicide that have discursively constructed the colonised as the inferior 'Other' of the superior European 'Self' (Lushaba and Lategan, 2019). Our decolonial approach proposes a formalised curriculum knowledge orientation that is decolonial and inclusive (Fanon, 1961). Following Fanon (1961, p. 45), we envisage a 'fully conscious human being free from coloniality and all its weakening effects'. As for the coloniser, we envisage a human being stripped from all biases and the weakening effects of the abyssal imperial attitudes (Madlingozi, 2018).

This book is founded on a bold proposition: to provide conceptual tools to inform the take-up of the decoloniality imperative within the curriculum. This task is based on what we have observed as a lacuna in the recent writings on decolonising education. Writing on decolonising education in South Africa since 2015 has focused almost exclusively on definitions and meanings. These writings turn on whether universities should favour a delinking type of argument that emphasises Africa-centred discourses and epistemologies. Debates also focus on whether decoloniality should be framed as part of broader inclusive ecologies of knowledge approach (de Sousa Santos, 2014). Writings on decoloniality centre a commitment to deep African precolonial history, the need to historicise African epistemic traditions, and specific articulations of the relationship between decolonial knowledge traditions and Africa-centredness.

Based on this quest for epistemological centring, we attempt to move the decolonial quest into the curriculum knowledge domain. We believe that such an emphasis is a requirement for concretely advancing the decolonisation of education. Without addressing the curriculum question, decolonisation will remain located at the symbolic level. In this case, it will struggle to impact the institutional curriculum of universities. Garuba (2015) called for such a development when he suggests that the decolonisation content to be studied must proceed based on critical modifications of the curriculum. In this light, Hapazari and Mkhize (2021, p. 109) argue persuasively that:

> Most African universities have not substantially transformed; hence, they continue to be grounded in colonial and Western epistemological traditions. By so doing, the colonialists have effectively instilled an inferiority complex in the Africans, and this complex is currently ingrained in their minds.

This book takes up the challenge of developing a theoretical approach to centring decoloniality into the university curriculum. We present what we call a knowledge-building approach to disciplines across the university's curriculum offerings, including the humanities, social sciences, natural sciences, and applied sciences. A knowledge-building approach is crucial for responding to the call to decolonise education. The book emphasises the importance of developing knowledge frames and approaches that can inform curriculum knowledge selection in cumulative and principled ways. In light of this, the chapters focus on developing an approach for inserting decolonial curriculum knowledge into knowledge-building processes in university curricula. The first three chapters offer perspectives on how decolonial curriculum knowledge could be contextualised and centred in university curricula. The final three chapters focus on knowledge-building approaches in specific disciplines. The book's commitment to curriculum knowledge across the curriculum is founded on the need to make careful distinctions about the precise nature of disciplinary knowledge in question in a specific curriculum knowledge field. The book provides an account of the conceptual basis on which these distinctions are made to guide decolonising the curriculum in specific disciplinary areas.

A realist approach

In this book, we are taking a realist approach. Knowledge is not simply socially constructed. Knowledge is a social attempt to describe a real mechanism operating in the world. Social sciences attempt to describe social mechanisms; natural sciences attempt to describe physical mechanisms (Price, 2019).

The first four chapters in this book, which are more focused on the social sciences and humanities, show in different ways how decoloniality involves both the critique of Eurocentric social concepts and an invitation to introduce concepts from the global South. This is important because the concepts point to real social mechanisms in the sense that they evidence more profound ways of thinking, valuing, and being. To reject a concept simply because of its source – for example, to throw out works by 'dead white men' or scholars from the global North – is to lose some insight into those mechanisms, such as where and how their knowledge was created and for what purposes (Fataar and Subreenduth, 2015). Although Eurocentric concepts have been forged in and through a Eurocentric worldview and may be unable to fully recognise and represent the epistemologies and ways of being of peoples with alternate worldviews, we can mount much more robust critiques if we engage in a realist manner with this knowledge. The chapter on the teaching of History (Chapter 5) illustrates the distortion of the colonial lens and the need to work away from this towards a more inclusive decolonial lens.

It is perhaps more difficult for those in the natural sciences to recognise the need for decolonisation. Whilst the concepts being taught describe a mechanism that exists independently of humanity and structure of human society (Price, 2019), natural science itself is a human activity. It is thus subject to power dynamics that exist in human societies. For example, the 'rational' and 'objective' so valued in natural science can easily unconsciously equate to an embodiment in a white, heterosexual, cis-gendered male. Thus, anyone who appears different must first prove themselves sufficiently 'rational' and 'objective' before their work is valorised.

If natural science is not Contextualised as a social activity, it cannot be recognised as having colonial or decolonial tendencies (Adendorff and Blackie, 2020). In the last two chapters of the book, we explore the nature of decoloniality in the natural sciences. A starting point for decolonising science is to recognise that particular human experiences shape thinking, and therefore a diversity of human experiences will benefit scientific progress.

One aspect of the unique contribution of this book that we have been able to illustrate is that the process of decolonisation will always be context dependent. Furthermore, part of the challenge is bridging the gap between the centring in the university's episteme on the one hand and developing curriculum and pedagogical tools for its context-sensitive incorporation into teaching and learning on the other. The use of established frameworks can facilitate this application within a particular university context. Whilst authors of the chapters in this book have drawn on multiple frameworks, most have drawn on Legitimation Code Theory (Maton, 2014, 2016, 2020) to varying extents.

Introducing Legitimation Code Theory (LCT)

Legitimation Code Theory (LCT) is described as a 'sociological framework motivated by social justice and knowledge-building issues' (Winberg *et al.*,

2020, p. 2). LCT is a framework comprising four sets of concepts or 'dimensions', of which Specialisation, Semantics, and Autonomy are enacted in this book. Each dimension comprises conceptual and analytical tools that enable analyses of different aspects of knowledge practices (Maton, 2016). In addition to analysing knowledge practices in curriculum, the use of these dimensions and their conceptual tools also affords us a means of achieving the kind of self-reflexivity that de Sousa Santos *et al.* (2007, p. xxi) hold as 'the first step towards the recognition of the epistemological diversity of the world'. For instance, in Chapter 5, the LCT dimension of Autonomy is used to show the imbalanced power relations that exist in the South African school history curriculum. These imbalanced power relations were traced from colonial-apartheid curricula to the post-colonial-apartheid curricula and have continued to produce a school history curriculum that is not epistemologically diverse. However, beyond this, LCT along with decolonial theory was used in this chapter to show how we can work towards transcending these imbalances towards a school history curriculum that is more epistemologically diverse.

Moreover, in Chapter 4, Hlatshwayo relies on the LCT concept of the 'epistemic – pedagogic device' (Maton, 2014) explore the different struggles that are happening in the calls for transformation and recontextualising,, he proposes that curriculum design and teaching and learning is not an innocent, neutral, and apolitical process. Rather, it is an important site that needs further exploring, critiquing, and challenging if we are to lodge a serious commitment to the transformation and recontextualisation of higher education.

Thus, although Western in genealogy, LCT offers a means of exploring, critiquing, and possibly addressing the power relations inherent in various meaning-making practices.

Authors in this volume employed various LCT tools, drawn from the dimensions of Autonomy (Chapter 4 and 6), Specialization (Chapters 3, 6, and 7) – including the 'epistemic plane' (Chapter 7), 'gazes' (Chapters 3 and 6), and the 'epistemic–pedagogic device' (Chapter 4) – and Semantics (Chapter 2). The epistemic–pedagogic device or 'EPD' theorises that different underpinning logics drive knowledge practices econtex through interconnected yet analytically distinct fields of production, recontextualisation, and reproduction. Acknowledging and working with such differences enabled authors using this conceptual tool to analytically separate and explore knowledge-building in the areas of research, curriculum design, and pedagogy (see Chapters 3 and 4).

The dimension of Autonomy focuses explicitly on power relations in different knowledge practices (Maton and Howard, 2018, 2021). Tools in this dimension conceptualise who the knowledge belongs to and to what end it is being used; it thus offers a way of exploring why some decolonisation attempts might fail, i.e., some of the curriculum renewal attempts discussed by Paul Maluleka and Neo Lekgotla *laga* Ramoupi in Chapter 5.

The dimension of Specialisation focuses on the relationship between knowledge and knowers in knowledge practices and differentiates fields based on whether and to what extent it is knowledge or knowers that is econtextu, neither or both equally. In this volume, the *epistemic plane* was used to highlight knower-blindness as a weak spot in natural science curricula (see Chapter 7). The *social plane* and the notion of developing a 'gaze' was used to look at the knower development over time (Chapter 3). The concept of *axiological constellations* (Maton, 2014) was used to help shed light on the decolonisation conversation in science. Constellation analysis looks at how ideas, objects, practices, and beliefs are organised and on what basis they are clustered together.

In this volume, importantly, we employ various decolonial concepts, frameworks, and tools that enable us to bring to light possibilities in recontextualising the university and its curriculum in post-colonial-apartheid South Africa with specific focus on curriculum knowledge-building. Thus, we also employ critical realism, Bernstein's 'pedagogic device', and LCT as theoretical lenses to highlight how they can be used to reposition the decolonial agenda underpinned by a sociological approach to education and knowledge that is vested in investigating the 'relations within' education and knowledge and their intrinsic structures towards addressing the knowledge question posed by the decolonial intellectual project (Lilliedahl, 2015). This posture is informed by a decoloniality that embraces ecologies of knowledge or pluriversity knowledge or post-abyssal epistemologies, and philosophy of Africanisation (de Sousa Santos, 2014; see Chapter 2 and 5). This 'is inspired by the current epistemic break' that seeks to break away 'from the knowledge that has been dominant for the past 500 years' (Sithole, 2014, p. 1). This is with the view of contributing to discourses that seek to reimagine and work towards building a university, curriculum, and education generally that are built on social, epistemological, and ontological justice. In this book, we argue that focusing on curriculum knowledge and the different epistemic possibilities that comes with foregrounding knowledge structures as well as making explicit the basis of achievement in curricula, is inherently transformative and decolonial as it opens up the curriculum spaces and does give (epistemological) access to students.

Chapter outline

Chapter 2 is by Aslam Fataar, who suggests that a knowledge-building approach is crucial for responding to the call to decolonise education.

Fataar's chapter aligns with the book's emphasis on the importance of developing knowledge frames and approaches that can inform curriculum knowledge selection. He develops an approach for inserting decolonial curriculum knowledge into knowledge-building processes in South African higher education. The chapter is based on the proposition that the commitment to knowledge and knowledge-building must be located within the cauldron of a highly contested South African higher education field. Fataar's chapter proceeds based on two inter-related arguments. The first is an attempt to discuss the decolonising knowledge imperative in the context of the prevailing politics of knowledge in higher education in South Africa. The second argument develops an 'educational knowledge' approach for guiding curriculum knowledge selection based on a decolonial approach.

Chapter 3 is by Kathy Luckett and provides a window into the lived experience of students and staff from the humanities. The tension between the importance of developing knowledge and the decolonial call for voices from the South is made visible using Specialisation. Luckett uses the relationship between the field of production, the field of recontextualisation and the field of reproduction mapped out in the epistemic-pedagogic device to show how a naïve approach to decoloniality can lead to an impoverished education, one that may be rich in the diversity of sources but unable to build decolonial knowledge adequately. Based on an analysis of the data for her chapter, Luckett proposes the development of three new gazes – the colonial, the decolonial, and the psychic. Using these gazes, one can see the variation in priorities around pedagogy and curriculum development, which has frequently led to miscommunication and discontent among those trying to find common ground. This chapter provides a conceptual foundation for advancing a realist approach to knowledge-building.

Chapter 4 is by Mlamuli Nkosingphile Hlatshwayo and draws on the epistemic–pedagogic device (EPD) to focus on the different struggles underlying calls for decolonising and transforming curricula in South African higher education. For Hlatshwayo, the EPD is a useful framework to understand the hidden coloniality, voices, ideology, and assumptions that often frustrate the potential for transformation in the academy. His chapter suggests that the field of recontextualisation (and its logics) should be seen as an important site for understanding different knowledge fields. This, according to Hlatshwayo, enables us to explore and foreground academics' ideology regarding what they deem to be valued and legitimate knowledge. Theorising these different fields can open the discursive space for decolonial and transformative interventions in higher education curricula.

Chapter 5, by Paul Maluleka and Neo Lekgotla *laga* Ramoupi. Is the first of three chapters that focus on curriculum knowledge-building in a specific discipline and subject. The chapter traces how the subject of School

History in the Further Education and Training (FET) phase in South Africa has been colonised since the colonial powers' formalised schooling. It then suggests ways in which the current School History Curriculum could be decolonised by adopting a critical decolonial conceptual framework and the dimension of Autonomy from LCT. By centring School History in debates around de/coloniality and Africanisation, the authors consciously seek to highlight the critical role that the discipline and subject of History at basic education level can play in the decolonial project and processes. This is because, in the main, emphasis on the need to decolonise curriculum is focused on university disciplines and subjects. Thus, school disciplines and subjects and their roles in the decolonial project tend to be ignored in the process. Hence, the authors believe that it would be futile to only speak of and only do decolonial work at the university level and neglect the basic education level.

Chapter 6, by Hanelie Adendorff and Margaret A.L. Blackie, uses *axiological constellations* to suggest ways in which the decolonial conversation in STEM disciplines can move beyond the code clash that has been highlighted in earlier work (Adendorff and Blackie, 2020). Drawing on the climate change work of Glenn (2015) as well as the authors' own experience with decolonisation conversations in STEM fields, the chapter offers two practical ways of translating or mediating the conversation. These are shifting the code of the message to that of the audience and using messengers who share the cosmology of the audience.

Chapter 7 is a companion piece to the previous chapter, by the same authors. Again, the focus is on decoloniality in tertiary science education. In this chapter, Blackie and Adendorff argue for the importance of consciously bringing the person into view in science education using tools from the dimension of Specialisation primarily. The centrality of knowledge tends to hold sway in STEM environments, but this tends to lead to an unconscious 'knower-blindness', i.e., the person of the scientist can be overlooked or downplayed in the quest for objectivity and reliable knowledge or 'truth'. Thus, the remedy for decoloniality in STEM education is not to replace scientific knowledge with traditional knowledge but to recognise the cultural embeddedness of science education. In other words, this chapter uses the epistemic plane from Specialisation to illustrate how junior scientists are trained and how who they as specialised knowers can be influential in how they 'do' science in their respective fields.

We offer the book in the spirit of ongoing debate and dialogue. We argue that an emphasis on curriculum knowledge is necessary for advancing the decolonial aims of education imperative. For this purpose, we introduced sets of knowledge-building tools to inform curriculum, teaching, and learning processes. We are not wedded to specific theoretical toolkits, yet LCT, we believe, offers robust 'languages' and 'frames' for decolonial curriculum insertion. It trains the decolonial spotlight centrally on the curriculum, which, from our perspective as education and curriculum scholars, is where we believe it matters most. The book is based on the assertion that recontextualisation of education would remain in the symbolic or discursive domain without a concerted cumulative curriculum knowledge-building approach. We offer the book as the first step in such an approach.

References

Adendorff, H. and Blackie, M. A. (2020) 'Decolonizing the science curriculum: When good intentions are not enough'. In C. Winberg, S. McKenna and K. Wilmot (Eds.), *Building knowledge in higher education: Enhancing teaching and learning with Legitimation Code Theory* (pp. 237–254). London: Routledge.

De Sousa Santos, B. (2014) *Epistemologies of the South: Justice against epistemicide.* Boulder, CO: Paradigm Publishers.

De Sousa Santos, B., Nunes, J. A. and Meneses, M. P. (2007) 'Opening up the canon of knowledge and recognition of difference'. In B. de Sousa Santos (Ed.), *Another knowledge is possible* (pp. xix–lxii). London: Verso.

Fanon, F. (1961) *The wretched of the earth* (Trans. By R. Philcox). New York: Grove Press.

Fataar, A. and Subreenduth, S. (2015) 'The search for ecologies of knowledge in the encounter with African epistemicide in South African education', *South African Journal of Higher Education, 29*(2), 106–121.

Garuba, H. (2015) 'What is an African curriculum?', *Mail and Guardian*, 17 April 2015. Retrieved from http://mg.co.za/article/2015-04-17-what-is-african-curriculum/

Hapazari, J. and Mkhize, G. (2021) 'Insights on the relevance of econtextua education in African higher education institutions and challenges posed by the COVID-19 pandemic', *African Perspectives of Research in Teaching and Learning, 5*(1), 108–125.

Lilliedahl, J. (2015) 'The recontextualisation of knowledge: Towards a social realist approach to curriculum and didactics', *Nordic Journal of Studies in Education Policy, 1*, 40–47.

Lushaba, L. and Lategan, Z. (2019) 'Review of *What is Africanness? Contesting nativism in race, culture and sexualities*', *Journal for Juridical Science, 44*(1), 139–144.

Madlingozi, T. (2018) *Mayibuye iAfrika? Disjunctive inclusions and black strivings for constitution and belonging in "South Africa"* (Doctoral thesis, Birkbeck College, University of London, London, United Kingdom). Retrieved from http://vufind.lib.bbk.ac.uk/vufind/Record/589681.

Maton, K. (2014) *Knowledge and knowers: Towards a realist sociology of education.* London: Routledge.

Maton, K. (2016) 'Legitimation Code Theory: Building knowledge about knowledge-building'. In K. Maton, S. Hood, and S. Shay (Eds.), *Knowledge-building: Educational studies in Legitimation Code Theory* (pp. 1–24). London: Routledge.

Maton, K. (2020) 'Semantic waves: Context, complexity and academic discourse'. In J. R. Martin, K. Maton and Y. J. Doran (Eds.) *Accessing academic discourse: Systemic functional linguistics and Legitimation Code Theory* (pp. 59–85). London: Routledge.

Maton, K. and Howard, S. K. (2018) 'Taking autonomy tours: A key to integrative knowledge-building', *LCT Centre Occasional Paper 1*, 1–35.

Maton, K. and Howard, S. K. (2021) 'Animating science: Activating the affordances of multimedia in teaching'. In K. Maton, J. R. Martin and Y. J. Doran (Eds.), *Teaching science: Knowledge, language, pedagogy* (pp. 76–102). London: Routledge.

Mbembe, A. (2016). 'Decolonizing the university: New directions', *Arts and Humanities in Higher Education*, *15*(1), 29–45.

Mohan, D. (2020) 'JNU and "safe spaces" under attack: Where will students go?', *The Quint*, 8 January 2020. Retrieved from www.thequint.com/voices/opinion/jnu-violence-student-politics-crackdown-activism-destruction-of-safe-spaces-education-

Ndlovu-Gatsheni, S. (2013) 'Decolonising the university in Africa', *The Thinker*, *51*, 46–51.

Price, L. (2019) 'The possibility of deep naturalism: A philosophy for ecology', *Journal of Critical Realism*, *18*, 352–367.

Sithole, T. (2014) *Achille Mbembe: Subject, subjection, and subjectivity* (Doctoral thesis, University of South Africa, Pretoria, South Africa). Retrieved from: http://uir.unisa.ac.za/bitstream/handle/10500/14323/thesis_sithole_t.pdf?sequence=1andisAllowed=y.

Tisani, N. C. (2018) 'Of definitions and naming: "I am the earth itself. God made me a chief on the very first day of creation"'. In J. Bam, L. Ntsebeza and A. Zinn (Eds.), *Whose history counts? Decolonising African pre-colonial historiography* (pp. 15–34). Cape Town: African Sun Media.

Winberg, C., McKenna, S. and Wilmot, K. (2020) '"Nothing so practical as good theory". Legitimation Code Theory in Higher Education'. In C. Winberg, S. McKenna and K. Wilmot (Eds.), *Building knowledge in higher Education: Enhancing Teaching and Learning with Legitimation Code Theory* (pp. 1–16). London: Routledge.

2 Pursuing decolonial knowledge-building in South African higher education

Aslam Fataar

This chapter suggests that a knowledge-building approach is crucial for responding to the call to decolonize education. It aligns with the book's emphasis on the importance of developing knowledge frames and approaches that can inform curriculum knowledge selection in cumulative and principled ways. In light of this, the chapter focuses on developing an approach for inserting decolonial curriculum knowledge into knowledge-building processes in South African higher education. The chapter is based on the proposition that the commitment to knowledge and knowledge-building must be located in the cauldron of a highly contested South African higher education field. I proceed based on two inter-related arguments. The first is an attempt to discuss the decolonizing knowledge imperative in the context of the prevailing politics of knowledge in higher education in South Africa. In this respect, I explore the conceptual terms on which a decolonial knowledge approach should be inserted into universities' epistemic schemata. This task, I argue, should be based on a commitment to knowledge as involving principled boundaried and cross-boundary constructions. The second argument, set out in the final section of the chapter, develops an 'educational knowledge' approach for guiding how curriculum knowledge selection would proceed based on a decolonial approach. Such a perspective, I contend, is crucial for moving the decolonial imperative forward productively into the arena of cumulative knowledge-building in higher education.

Colonialism, apartheid, and the residue of exclusionary curriculum knowledge

Since the official end of apartheid in 1994, South Africa has struggled to shift from an exclusionary colonial social structure to one that has become formally, if not substantively, inclusive. In pursuing substantive, socially just inclusion, educational sectors appear at once to be sites of necessary

DOI: 10.4324/9781003106968-2

possibility and seeming impossibility. While the country's schools and universities have experienced limited demographic integration, more inclusive demographics have not meant a more inclusive curriculum.

South Africa has been an important laboratory for debates about the nature of educational provision and curricular forms, specifically as they developed from (Dutch and British) colonial times into the apartheid and post-apartheid periods. Questions about appropriate knowledge orientations for the former local colonial populations have remained central to curriculum debates and policy discourses. These concerns have been raised in the light of broader questions about the nature of the humanness of the colonial native, which in turn have raised, as their corollary, questions about policy projections for the most suitable curriculum forms. These questions emerged sharply in the South African educational discourse between 1920 and the 1950s in response to the anxieties experienced by the politically hegemonic white polity concerning the appropriate form of education for blacks. This apprehension was in turn rooted in the desire to retain white privilege in the face of increasing black urbanization, which was accompanied by the demand from the disenfranchised black population for racial parity, modernization, and social justice.

A confluence of local and international discursive transfer modalities between the Anglo-American world, on the one hand, and white education policymakers in the South African (post)colony during the first half of the twentieth century, on the other, centred on the nature of curriculum provision for the black native populations (see Cross, 1986; Hunt and Davis, 1976). These modalities were suffused with academic and political considerations about the appropriate form of education for blacks. For example, Charles T. Loram, an American-trained South African liberal and influential educational bureaucrat and policy expert, conceded that Africans suffered from genuine social and economic disabilities. However, he viewed them as not yet mature enough in their stage of development to warrant a fully modern Western education. Believing that Africans were a subject race in need of betterment, Loram suggested 'that there should be a reasonable outlet for the educated Native to earn an honest living, to dwell under decent conditions and to have some voice in the management of his affairs' (Loram, 1921, p. 505). Deriving his perspectives on schooling for blacks from, among others, American models of black education in the American South, such as the Tuskegee programmes – he had studied at Teachers College Columbia University – Loram asserted that 'we should take cognizance of the danger . . . of educating any number of individuals beyond the requirements of their race (1917, p. 310). He suggested that all that Africans required was an elementary education geared towards their everyday needs (see Hunt Davis, 1976, p. 96).

During the 1940s and 1950s, Afrikaner nationalist policymakers framed black education along rigid exclusionary lines in tandem with the Afrikaners' adherence to a discourse of racial purity as a means of addressing the social and economic impoverishment of its Afrikaner constituency (Kros, 2010). They suggested that black societies should undergo a Christian transformation but retain their essential 'Bantu' tribal character and emphasized the need to preserve the intrinsic qualities of African culture and maintain teaching in the mother tongue. They supported a form of education that would demonstrate that racial and educational segregation was aimed at developing a racially authentic character (see Cross, 1986, pp. 186–188). It is clear that the relationship between a particular view of black South Africans' social and cultural character directly impacted the educational and curricular forms favoured by successive white governments during the twentieth century. This found its most pernicious expression in the instantiation of the curriculum under the apartheid curriculum, which aimed to maintain blacks' racial subordination.

The social character of this subordinating curriculum has led South African education theorist, Crain Soudien, to argue that 'social difference, as opposed to, say, pedagogical reform is the central question that drives curriculum development in South and Southern Africa' (2010, p. 20). This view suggests that colonial and apartheid educational discourses were worked out on the basis of a specific conceptualization of the production of putative social identities of people, which in turn informed governmental curriculum policy orientations; in the case of British colonialism, an adapted curriculum was based on keeping blacks at a lower level of functional civility, and later the apartheid curriculum was focused on the production of racial and ethnic identities of subordination. It is, therefore, no coincidence that conceptions of social difference, especially the democratic project of transformation and social inclusion, have taken centre stage in post-apartheid South Africa, although as Veracini, writing in a different post-colonial context, reminds us, 'the configuration of settler political domination may have been superseded, but many of the discursive regimes that underpinned its constitution have remained in place' (2012, p. 326). Clearly then, radical social inclusion has had to contend with discursive continuities from earlier times.

The post-apartheid curriculum became a key political platform for undoing the legacy of racial exclusion and for generating a democratic citizenry, albeit in a context of contestation about the suitable curricular orientation for such a project. Put differently, such contestation has pivoted primarily on the proper articulation of conceptions of social justice, in terms of which the post-apartheid curriculum should be implemented. A key element of these contestations is a consideration of the most appropriate curriculum orientation that would undo the racist legacy of the past. Soudien (2010, p. 20) illustrates key impulses at play in the history of the country's curricular debates by explaining that,

> Curriculum development processes in the southern African region and other parts of the globe involve a forceful incorporation into the dominant structures of the world. This incorporation is an insistently ambiguous process precipitating . . . moments of both oppression and freedom. The weight of colonial oppression cannot be equated with the small opportunity yielded by it, but its internal contradictions, inherent to it, are what we should be alert to.

This suggests that a vision of oppression and freedom inherent in these small opportunities found in the interstices of (post)colonial or (post)apartheid discourses, structures and practices would provide the ontological basis for the epistemological underpinnings of the curriculum via an openness to the attendant knowledge-generation practices and knowledges of subordinate peoples. Such a perspective has, however, failed to emerge substantively as a curriculum orientation in South African education during the post-apartheid period. It was stymied by the instrumentalization associated with governmental curriculum policy and the ensuing institutional practices in the country's schools and universities. Its overriding curriculum knowledge approach was trumped by an instrumentalist orientation based on narrowly prescribing pedagogical outcomes for curricular achievement.

This was notwithstanding the South African government's policy attempt to accord its curriculum framework, through its outcomes-based education curricular approach, a multi-dimensional view of knowledge based on a critical appropriation of the human knowledges of oppressed populations. This framework was based on an attempt to allow the curriculum to accord credence to the everyday knowledges of people in the school curriculum. Such a knowledge perspective broke down due to its inchoate conceptual architecture and the massive problems experienced with implementation in schools across the entire country (see Fataar, 2006). Its valorization of marginal groups' knowledge and points of view was undermined by a concomitant lack of a curriculum framework to develop and inform curriculum knowledge and pedagogical work. It is therefore clear that, while the decolonial imperative has recently been asserted politically by students and some academics, the conceptual space for centring a decolonial approach in the institutional curriculum remains very small, and this task is made no less difficult by the lack of knowledge-building approaches to work decoloniality into the curriculum.

Decolonizing education (DE) in the context of South Africa's higher education politics of knowledge

Calls to decolonize education have been circulating in university circles since the Rhodes and Fees Must Fall protests of 2015–2016. These calls have been accompanied by energetic arguments, mainly in the popular media and online news platforms, conducted by various players, including educational commentators and student leaders. The general call has been for a curricular approach that challenges the Western Eurocentric knowledge approaches that have dominated university knowledge and education more generally. Knowledge that challenges and overturns the Western canon, emphasizing an 'all inclusive' approach to planetary knowledges, an ecologies type of knowledge approach, has been inserted into the centre of our public and educational discourses. We have not yet seen any large-scale curriculum changes on this basis at our universities or schools, despite some documents in support put out by the national Department of Basic Education and the Centre on Higher Education, as well as policy activity in teaching and learning at a few universities, small-scale curriculum initiatives, and many university symposia and workshops. The South African Education Research Association has focused prominently on the DE imperative during four consecutive annual conferences since 2015. We have, however, not seen the emergence of a concerted body of academic work that considers the conceptual or scholarly bases on which a decolonized educational system and associated curriculum offerings would be established.

A limited set of academic papers sought to insert the DE call as a knowledge project into the academic domain. Articles by Mbembe (2016) and Ndlovu-Gatsheni (2013) stake out some outlines of the debate, the former favouring an Afropolitan decolonial approach and the latter arguing for a type of Africa-centred orientation. Others such as Heleta (2016) has also made a significant contribution to this nascent debate emphasizing Afrocentrism. Jansen (2017) argues that the DE debate signals the latest incarnation of South Africa's preponderance of 'policy as symbols', thereby skirting issues of substantive curriculum reform. He suggests that there is a naïveté about how this debate is pursued, which is not based on current scholarship associated with curriculum research and theory, nor on a realistic understanding of the dynamics of curriculum reform.

The call to decolonize education ought to be understood as the latest articulation of contestation around the 'politics of knowledge' in South Africa since the mid-1990s, with its roots in the apartheid period. A politics of knowledge emphasizes the external political dimensions of knowledge, not its internal discursive grammars. Such a contest occurred alongside the instantiation of particular sets of curriculum approaches in governmental education policy and institutional curriculum offerings, especially the generic competence-based regime in schooling policy, as evinced in Curriculum 2005 and the integrated qualifications approach in further and higher education (see Fataar, 2006). The larger educational and university restructuring processes during the late 1990s occurred around the governmentally authorized qualifications policy discourse that favoured generic curricula to be delivered via university programmes. Qualifications approaches favoured greater alignment with professional and occupational sectors, and universities were called on to produce graduates for the workplace. As illustrated by the government's Curriculum 2005, drawing on an outcomes-based approach to the school curriculum, a discourse of competence and generic skills-based learning had come to dominate the education reform agenda and crept into higher education through universities' moves to adopt programmes of learning with linkages to the world of work.

In light of this, the old question of 'what knowledge is of worth' raised by C.P. Snow in the United Kingdom during the 1950s, and much earlier by Herbert Spencer in the 1860s, in which he questioned the dominance of the humanities over the sciences and professional knowledge, began to get academic attention (Herbert, 2013). The question here is about the specific role and nature of knowledge in the curriculum. A critique of the collapse of everyday or horizontal knowledge into specialized vertical knowledge entered the terrain of the politics of knowledge, which underpinned the faltering attempt during the early 2000s to 'walk' educational policy and institutional discourses back from the competence-dominated genericism embedded in the school curriculum and university programmes.

A debate that demonstrated this struggle occurred at UCT in the late 2000s around a professorial inaugural address by physical anthropologist Alan Morris, whose provocatively titled address, 'The politics of old bones', elicited discussion about the nature of university knowledge and the role of disciplines. Morris argued that his discipline had been negatively impacted by the denial of the science of biology in understanding human variation, having come under attack from the social sciences that such biological variation does not exist. Such a perspective, he argued, was developed on the basis of the discredited concept of race. Morris argued that 'there is a myth among social sciences that because physical anthropology no longer accepts the concept of race, that human variation somehow doesn't exist' (Morris, 2008, p. 3). The empirical case that Morris used to demonstrate his argument in support of the biological study of human bones was the vexed question of the exhumation of human bones at a graveyard in downtown Cape Town. Controversy erupted around the exhumation pushed for by developers in the light of the slave and indigenous origins of those buried on the site.

Martin Hall, an ex-archaeology professor at UCT, launched a scathing critique of Morris's attempt to privilege human biology in studying the skeletons. Morris applied to the South African Heritage Resources Agency for permission to study the skeletons on the basis that he would be able to show 'how we could decipher a wealth of information about health, lifestyle and demography from the skeletons' (Morris, 2008, p. 3). Hall accused Morris of peddling a misinformed attempt to 'control the production of knowledge in terms of a simple dichotomy between science and society' (Hall, 2009, p. 71). Based on an application of Actor-Network Theory, Hall went on to argue that at least three knowledge constellations were circulating around this vexed issue. Each constellation was informed by interactions among knowledge generation, networked interests, and the mobilizing of resources. He distinguished between the three knowledge discourses at play, viz. the discourses of development, memory, and science, each operating on a specific 'legitimating view of an integrated world – and each would claim to represent a larger group . . . and each is aligned directly or indirectly with a set of academic disciplines' (2009, p. 71). Hall's larger point is that each constellation is based on a system of circulating reference, which it brings into the analytical picture, which, in turn, makes the opposition between 'science' and 'society' redundant. Hall offers the view that in attempting to find out more about the worlds of underclass urban communities, such as of those buried at the Cape Town site, for example, 'it should be possible to map out an [interdisciplinary] approach that would result in a productive intersection between these [hitherto] distinct networks' (2009, p. 74).

The debate that ensued between Hall and Joe Muller, a leading South African sociologist of knowledge, illuminates the contending perspectives on the nature of disciplinary knowledge in the university, which, in my estimation, the insertion of a decolonial knowledge approach would also have to contend with. In other words, such an approach is a subset of a larger debate in respect of which the 'knowledge of the university' ought to be understood and conceptualized. Muller bases his views on the need to properly account for the varieties of specialized knowledge and their boundaries in the university and to recognize the idea of expertise. He suggests that not all discourses carry the same epistemic weight. I take this to mean that biological knowledge has a conceptual structure that is distinct from, for example, historical knowledge with its own different knowledge structure, which characterizes its propositional and procedural forms of knowledge and the research methods that are put to work in these respective knowledge domains. Muller suggests that collapsing the boundary between distinctive knowledge structures would occlude what knowledge is operative in a knowledge constellation. Hence Muller's retort to Hall is that 'if this [collapse of boundaries] is taken to mean that all discourses [structures] carry the same socio-epistemic "weight", then we part company. Denying, ignoring or downplaying socio-epistemic "weight" can have serious consequences' (Muller, 2009a, p. 80).

Hall demurs because he is interested in working across the binary between different knowledge discourses. He rejects the charge against him that he thinks that different knowledge systems have equal or the same socio-epistemic weight. He explains that there is 'no inherent reason why two (Science and Memory) systems of circulation should be in conflict, since their ultimate interests are different' (Hall, 2009, p. 86). According to Hall, scientists are motivated by the reputational benefits associated with publication and citation, and memory work attempts to valorize the lives of the underclasses. While Muller's position is in support of disciplinary knowledge sanctified by the inner community of scholars, Hall objects to an *a priori* status conferred on 'institutions and disciplines to the protection of their boundaries by arguing that not adhering to such a boundaried view of knowledge would allow for new knowledge possibilities to become evident' (Hall, 2009, p. 86).

It is my view that arguing for a DE perspective would have to account for a careful distillation of these two positions; on the one hand, it should observe the proper, not equal, socio-epistemic weight that attends to and is operative in disciplinary knowledge structures, their internal community of scholars, research protocols, and allegiances to specific methods and prior knowledge claims. Such a position is advanced by Bernstein's emphasis on the epistemic differences between horizontal and vertical discourses (Bernstein, 1999), where care has to be taken when working with horizontal or everyday knowledge to avoid the pitfalls of undermining or obfuscating the verticality of knowledge discourses. Specialization is key to knowledge at the university. Similarly, within vertical discourses, the distinction between vertical and horizontal knowledge structures is important in understanding, for example, the difference between the internal vertical knowledge or grammar of physical science or chemistry and the internal segmental or horizontal grammar of sociology or political science.

On the other hand, the interaction between different knowledge constellations, as supported by Hall, opens up the possibility for carefully working across different knowledge structures, as, for example, in the way that Zipin (2017) conceptualizes what he calls 'knowledge problematics'. Zipin does not favour an unboundaried view based on the collapse of science and community funds of knowledge in his example of addressing water management in flooded zones. What he argues for, instead, is a calibrated conversation between these two knowledge discourses (science and community) in addressing a specific problem or need in society. Zipin draws on the work of Whatmore and Landström (2011, cited in Zipin, 2017) to distil from their work strategic principles for curriculum work, which he draws on to illustrate how the scientific community is able to explain the science of weather, ground erosion, and flooding, while the local community contributes applied knowledge of weather and flooding patterns and their effects in a problem-resolving approach to addressing the problems associated with flooding in low-lying areas of their town. The combination of distinct and complementary knowledge structures made up of scientists, on the one hand, and community knowledge experts and laypeople, on the other hand, enabled such a problematics-based approach to generate a new knowledge-informed consensus that guided the community's approach to dealing with flooding. This is an expression of the type of new knowledge that Hall refers to that would emerge out of bringing distinctive knowledge discourses into a focused conversation where they complement each other. This is done without according *equal* socio-epistemic worth to the different knowledge constellations; in fact, observing disciplinary structures and boundaries, as I explain in the following sections, is key to putting different knowledge constellations into conversation with each other.

I argue that a decolonial knowledge approach has to consider the politics of knowledge that I describe earlier. The DE imperative emerged out of what students experienced as their deep institutional misrecognition at the post-apartheid university. Students petitioned against the misrecognition embedded in the knowledge they were inducted into at the university, which they argued, failed to recognize, valorize, and engage their African-located identifications. They argued that the domination of Western-centred knowledge was central to their educational misrecognition (see Fataar, 2018). The students, therefore, fundamentally challenged the university's key message systems of curriculum, assessment and pedagogy, which the knowledge contestations of the last three decades that I describe earlier failed to address appropriately. Shortcomings in the university's epistemic structures have been laid bare. In light of this, I argue that one productive response to such a challenge is to develop a decolonial approach based on careful consideration of its potential operations in the selection of curriculum knowledge.

The following section concentrates on the different knowledge claims of decoloniality, i.e., what type of knowledge claims are involved in decoloniality and how might these be incorporated into the higher education curriculum at the university.

Decoloniality and curriculum knowledge selection

In this section, I move the debate to a consideration of the epistemological claims of a decoloniality approach and, based on this, discuss how decoloniality would inform curriculum knowledge selection at the university.

Universities are complex systems with different knowledge mixes operating across *different knowledge regions*, i.e., disciplinary, applied, vocational, and professional knowledge. Each of these has its own knowledge structures, a theoretical understanding of which would provide a basis for working out how an approach to decoloniality would inform curriculum selection processes.

This section of the chapter is based on a conceptual toolkit to inform curriculum selection processes that I call an 'educational knowledge' approach to decolonizing the curriculum. For this purpose, I draw on two theoretical families that have hitherto operated on parallel and incommensurate epistemological tracks. I place the theoretical literature on decoloniality into conversation with knowledge-building literature on conceptions of 'educational (curriculum) knowledge'.

The section is made up of three sets of comments to develop my argument. The first set is a consideration of the curriculum knowledge claims of the decolonizing approach. Decoloniality is based on a critique of the formative relationship between the coloniality of power, knowledge, and being (see Maldonado-Torres, 2007). The triumph of modern colonial epistemology, it argues, was achieved through colonial violence, the relegation of people's knowledges to an inferior status, and the creation of the deracinated modern colonial subject. Race is central to colonial epistemology (Ndlovu-Gatsheni, 2013).

Decoloniality can be understood as a call for cognitive justice based on an overhaul and expansion of the Western knowledge canon. The call is also for knowledge pluralization, which refers to incorporating the complex ways of knowing of subaltern and all previously excluded groups (Fataar and Subreenduth, 2015). It favours an inter-cultural understanding of heterodox forms of being human. All knowledge forms have to be brought into play in an intercultural education that promotes a type of epistemic openness to the knowledges of all human beings. Despite accusations of being caught up in 'obsolete' knowledge of the past, decoloniality is focused on the complex challenges that characterize our posthuman condition. Questions about emerging life forms in the wake of climate change, artificial intelligence, and technological innovation take centre stage in their dynamic interaction with decoloniality. The call for DE is thus nothing less than the full incorporation of all of humanity's knowledge systems, past, present, and in anticipation of future knowledge constellations, into the knowledge selection systems of universities. But not all knowledge can logically be included in the curriculum. What is required is knowledge selection through the contingent curriculum processes of specific university programmes and modules.

Decoloniality, I argue, offers three curriculum knowledge claims. *Claim one*, as illustrated earlier, is based on *the centring of an all-inclusive, ecologies of knowledge approach* (Santos, 2014) that challenges the hegemony of Eurocentric theories, concepts, canons, and perspectives. *Claim two* is the *knowledge and identity claim*, based on the productive recognition and restoration of the full dignity of subjugated peoples and so unearths their full human potential. And, *claim three* pivots on *knowledge relevance and contextualization*. This is the idea that curriculum knowledge ought to make epistemological connections to people's knowledges, contextual life circumstances, indigenous knowledge systems, literacies, languages, and ways of knowing. This claim emphasizes the dynamism embedded in the connections made to the contexts and knowledges of people's Africa-centred lifeworlds (see Zipin, 2017, Cooper and Morrell, 2014). I attend to each of these three claims – *centring knowledge, knowledge and identity, and knowledge relevance* – in the following sections.

For my second argument set, I appropriate what has come to be called a knowledge-building approach to educational (curriculum) knowledge. Knowledge-building provides us with a set of theoretical tools to inform curriculum selection. The core challenge here is to work with theoretical families with different approaches to identifying knowledge boundaries; social realism requires observation of knowledge boundaries and the socio-epistemic weight of disciplines, while decoloniality insists on a flexible, principled, complementary cross-boundary approach.

Knowledge-building emphasizes a real(ist) conception of knowledge, not a constructivist one. A realist conception makes the point that any discipline has a basic conceptual scheme by which its knowledge is organized and grows. Social realists call these schemes knowledge structures. They point out that knowledge structures are either vertical as in physics and chemistry with a strong spine of tightly linked internal concepts, or horizontal as in sociology and political science, whose schemes are characterized by sets of concepts that develop segmentally (see Young, 2008). However, as explained in the previous section, these knowledge structures are not binary either/or, or self-enclosed systems. Both sets of knowledge structures, as I argued earlier, allow fertile space for inserting decoloniality, although in different ways depending on how one works with the logic of their structures.

Subject areas such as sociology, journalism, and marketing, for example, would facilitate a decolonial turn by including different and ever-expanding sets of theories and bodies of social knowledge to offer greater, more inclusive objectivity. In this way, it becomes possible to 'pursue a robust social science by triangulating a wide range of partial perspectives, which would yield "stronger objectivity" than the "God trick" of supposed objectification from a dis-interested universal perspective' (Haraway, 1988 as developed in Zipin *et al.* , 2015, p. 16).

The space to decolonize vertical knowledge structures (e.g., science) could be opened up by highlighting, for example, the historical development of mathematics, astronomy, and medical concepts. This would be done through incorporating hitherto ignored scientific work from India, Africa, and Asia, where many of the foundations of these disciplines were laid. Decolonizing science-related disciplines such as chemistry and physics would emphasize how they evolve and subsist through their historical, contextual, and horizontal integration with the social world via the social sciences, emphasizing what Santos (2014) calls the 'external plurality' of science. Decoloniality here would thus work carefully and principally through dismantling the silos of knowledge structures. Moreover, a decolonial approach would also emphasize what Santos (2014) calls the 'internal plurality' of scientific knowledge based on the view that, over time, 'scientific research developed on a complex mix of science and non-science constructs; the selection of topics, problems, theoretical models, methodologies, languages, images, and forms of argument' (2014, p. 194).

Decolonizing knowledge in the areas of history and social theory could include, for example, the work of Ibn Khaldun on 'assabiyyah' (social structures and cohesion) developed in the fourteenth century in the Maghreb region of Africa (Alatas, 2006) and ubuntu-inspired social and philosophical work developed in South Africa in recent years (Letseka, 2013). Ibn Khaldun's theoretical architecture precedes the social structuralism of scholars such as Karl Marx, Claude Lévi-Strauss, and Pierre Bourdieu. And ubuntu-inspired philosophy provides fruitful ground for working with the context-related cosmological knowledges of people. Ibn Khaldun's assabiyah and ubuntu could be incorporated into the knowledge structuring of history, law, sociology, public administration, philosophy, and business management curricula. Such perspectives would extend our theoretical frameworks, in addition to introducing students to a much broader epistemological canon.

Similarly, in disciplines such as history, literature, and law, one could work with different periodizations and conceptions of world and African history and society, which would challenge constructions that emerged from colonial discourse. The unilinear depiction of modernity as an Enlightenment phenomenon could be problematized through a consideration of multiple models of modernity that emphasize how slavery, war, capital, bureaucracies, education, and other social systems worked in Africa, Asia, and the Americas before, during, and after the onset of colonial or imperial modernity.

The South American scholar, Enrique Dussel, introduces the notion of trans-modernity that brings a pluriversal understanding of modernity into view. He explains that 'trans-modernity is a recognition of epistemic diversity without epistemic relativism' (in Grosfoguel, 2013, p. 88). Such a perspective breaks with a universalist view where only Western men (sic) define what counts as knowledge. The centring of an all-inclusive ecologies of knowledge approach, based on a trans-modern pluriversal view, I argue, would thus be facilitated by adopting a principled approach to curriculum selection that respects the knowledge structures brought into play within the specificity of particular curriculum constellations at the university.

My third and final argument set moves explicitly to address principles of decolonizing curriculum selection with respect to some of the university's knowledge regions. Shay (2013) builds on Muller's (2009b) discussion of knowledge differentiation to bring curriculum selection in professional and vocational education into view. She uses the distinction offered by Legitimation Code Theory, specifically between the concepts of *semantic gravity* (relative context-dependence of meanings) and *semantic density* (relative condensation of meaning within concepts and symbols) in the dimension of Semantics (Maton, 2013) to guide her theorizing.

Drawing on Shay (2013), I suggest that the relative strength or weakness of a discipline's logical coherence with respect to concepts (*semantic density*) as well as the relative strength or weakness of its coherence with respect to context (*semantic gravity*) would allow one to determine how to incorporate decoloniality into specific knowledge constellations. The question that has to be asked is how a specific knowledge area's conceptual coherence and contextual coherence come together in its knowledge offering. This is not an either/or proposition. In other words, no field of knowledge is founded entirely on either contextual or conceptual knowledge. A knowledge area is constituted in a specific manner depending on the interplay between its contextual and conceptual knowledge dimensions.

I argue that the decolonial appeal for the contextual relevance of knowledge would find space in those knowledge areas or subjects with more significant contextual purchase and application, in other words, where the logic of the discipline is derived from its context.

The example of the subject, design, which resides in the area of vocational or professional education, illustrates the possibilities for an emphasis on decolonial relevance (see Gilio and Belluigi, 2017). Design is conceptually informed by its external relation to people's lived contexts from where it derives its logical principles. Active interaction with local Africa-centred aesthetics, knowledges, languages, architectures, and tastes is paramount in how the 'knowledge for design' is recontextualized into the curriculum. There is a particular relationship between context and concepts. The curriculum logic for design is derived from the context of its application, and recontextualization into the curriculum occurs through a process of concept development that derives from the contexts. The concepts are developed with reference to the logic of the contexts.

This would also apply to disciplines such as engineering, agriculture, bio-informatics and commercial law. The knowledge assemblages of these disciplines are defined by conceptual logics that are worked out in respect of their application in professional and vocational contexts. While not deriving their primary logics from contexts, as is the case of design, curriculum selection in these areas would emphasize how their disciplinary and conceptual logics would apply to their African and decolonial contexts of application. This is a somewhat truncated account, but the point I wish to make is that understanding the specific relationship between concepts and contexts in specific knowledge regions and their recontextualization in the curriculum opens up the possibility of careful and disciplined incorporation of the principles of decoloniality and Africa-centred relevance into specific curriculum areas.

Conclusion

This chapter has located the quest for decolonizing knowledge and the curriculum in the exclusionary and discriminatory logics of the colonial and apartheid curriculum. It offered a discussion of the politics of knowledge in South African higher education, especially key debates about how the knowledge question has been approached in light of calls to decolonize the curriculum. I proffered an argument for the necessity of a principled boundaried and cross-boundaried approach that would provide space to bring decoloniality into the full knowledge relations of the university. I offered an argument for a decolonial educational knowledge approach that would enable academics to insert decoloniality into the various disciplinary and multi-disciplinary curriculum knowledge regions of the university.

Incorporating a decolonial approach into the university curriculum is not easy. There is much work to be done. Frames and concepts have to be developed and research pursued for decoloniality to inform curriculum selection. Such a task invites us to bring new knowledge problems and trans- and inter-disciplinary work into curriculum design. A related focus would be on other equally important curriculum processes such as pedagogy and assessment. This chapter has suggested that working with and developing 'educational knowledge' concepts would help us move decoloniality into the space of curriculum knowledge selection.

References

Alatas, F. (2006) 'Ibn Khaldun and contemporary Sociology', *International Sociology, 21*(6), 782–795.

Bernstein, B. (1999) 'Vertical and horizontal discourses: An essay', *British Journal of Sociology of Education*, *20*(2), 157–173.

Cooper, D. and Morrell, R. (Eds.). (2014) *Africa-centred knowledges: Crossing fields and worlds*. New York: James Currey.

Cross, M. (1986) 'A historical review of education in South Africa: Towards an assessment', *Comparative Education*, *22*(3), 185–200.

Fataar, A. (2006) 'Policy networks in recalibrated terrain: The case of school curriculum policy and policy in South Africa', *Journal of Education Policy*, *21*(6), 641–659.

Fataar, A. (2018) 'Placing students at the centre of the decolonizing education imperative: Engaging the (mis)recognition struggles of students at the post-apartheid university', *Educational Studies*, *54*(6), 595–608.

Fataar, A. and Subreenduth, S. (2015) 'The search for ecologies of knowledge in the encounter with African epistemicide in South African education', *South African Journal of Higher Education*, *29*(2), 106–121.

Gilio, S. and Belluigi, D. (2017) 'Underlying knowledge – knower structures in graphic design: Contributing to establishing a cohesive language for use in graphic design education', *Art, Design and Communication in Higher Education*, *16*(2), 7–21.

Grosfoguel, R. (2013) 'The structure of knowledge in Westernized universities: Epistemic racism/sexism and the four genocides/epistemicides of the long 16th century', *Human Architecture: Journal of the Sociology of Self-Knowledge*, *XI*(1), 73–89.

Hall, M. (2009) 'New knowledge and the university', *Anthropology South Africa*, *32*(1 and 2), 69–76.

Haraway, D. (1988) 'The science question in feminism and the privilege of partial perspective', *Feminist Studies*, *14*(3), 575–599.

Heleta, S. (2016) 'Decolonization of higher education: Dismantling epistemic violence and Eurocentrism in South Africa', *Transformation in Higher Education*, *1*(1), 1–8.

Herbert, S. (2013) *What knowledge is of most worth*. TheClassics.us.

Hunt Davis, R. (1976) 'Charles T. Loram and an American model for African education in South Africa', *African Studies Review*, *19*(2), 87–99.

Jansen, J. (2017) 'Decolonising the university given a dysfunctional school system', *Journal of Education*, *68*, 3–13.

Kros, C. (2010) *The seeds of separate development: Origins of Bantu Education*. Pretoria: Unisa Press.

Letseka, M. (2013) 'Educating for Ubuntu/Botho: Lessons from Basotho indigenous education', *Open Journal of Philosophy*, *3*(2), 337–344.

Loram, C. (1917) *The education of the South African native*. London: Longmans, Green and Company.

Loram, C. (1921) 'The Phelps-Stokes Education Commission in South Africa', *International Review of Missions*, *10*, 496–508.

Maldonado-Torres, N. (2007) 'On the coloniality of being', *Cultural Studies*, *21*(2–3), 240–270.

Maton, K. (2013) 'Making semantic waves: A key to cumulative knowledge-building', *Linguistics and Education*, *24*(1), 8–22.

Mbembe, A. (2016) 'Decolonizing the university: New directions', *Arts and Humanities in Higher Education*, *5*(1), 29–45.

Morris, A. (2008) 'The politics of old bones'. Inaugural lecture in the Faculty of Health Sciences, University of Cape Town, 14 October, 2008. Retrieved from www.uct.ac.za/downloads/uct.ac.za/news/lectures/inaugurals/Alan_Morris.pdf

Muller, J. (2009a) 'Burning the straw man: A response to hall', *Anthropology South Africa*, *32*(1 and 2), 78–79.

Muller, J. (2009b) 'Forms of knowledge and curriculum coherence', *Journal of Education and Work*, *22*(3), 205–226.

Ndlovu-Gatsheni, S. (2013) 'Why decoloniality in the 21st century?', *The Thinker*, *48*, 10–15.

Santos, B. (2014) *Epistemologies of the South: Justice against epistemicide*. Boulder: Paradigm Publishers.

Shay, S. (2013) 'Conceptualizing curriculum differentiation in higher education: A sociology of knowledge point of view', *British Journal of Sociology of Education*, *34*(4), 563–582.

Soudien, C. (2010) ' "What to teach the natives": A historiography of the curriculum dilemma in South Africa'. In W. Pinar (Ed.), *Curriculum studies in South Africa: Intellectual histories and present circumstances* (pp. 19–49). New York: Palgrave Macmillan.

Veracini, L. (2012) 'Settler colonialism: A global and contemporary phenomenon', *Arena Journal*, *37/38*, 322–336.

Whatmore, S. and Landström, C. (2011) 'Flood apprentices: An exercise in making things public', *Economy and Society*, *40*(4), 582–610.

Young, M. (2008). Bringing knowledge back in: From social construction to social realism in the sociology of education. New York. Routledge.

Zipin, L. (2017) 'Pursuing a problematic-based curriculum approach for the sake of social justice', *Journal of Education*, *69*, 67–92.

Zipin, L., Fataar, A. and Brennan, M. (2015) 'Can social realism do social justice? Debating the warrants for curriculum knowledge selection', *Education as Change*, *19*(2), 9–36.

3 Building a 'decolonial knower'

Contestations in the humanities

Kathy Luckett

Introduction

This chapter discusses contestations around the 'decolonial turn' and interpretations of its meaning for institutionalized knowledge and curriculum in South African higher education, with a focus on the humanities disciplines. To do this I zoom in and analyze calls to 'decolonize the curriculum' and responses to that call at one university during and after the student protests (2015–2017). I argue that in a post-colonial context, still burdened with a legacy of education based on 'colonial difference' (Chatterjee, 2011), calls to decolonize knowledge, the curriculum, and pedagogy can be understood as a set of counter-claims by subaltern knowers desiring 'liberation' from the domination and control of knowledge production by knowers, institutions, and languages of European origin. Struggles around what and whose knowledge, what practices and whose dispositions should count in higher education fields in the South are also strategic moves for status and resources by those whose dispositions and practices have been discounted or misrecognized hitherto and who, consequently, have experienced marginalization or exclusion from the academic game.

Following Foucault's analysis of the French student protests in May 1968 as a moment of 'contingent eventualization' that opened-up a 'line of fragility' based on a 'breach of self-evidence (Foucault, 2000, pp. 226–227), I suggest similarly that the recent student protests can be understood as a 'ruptural' event in the constitution of the modern (post)-colonial historically white South Africa university. For Foucault,

> It means making visible a singularity at places where there is a temptation to invoke a historical constant, an immediate anthropological trait, or an obviousness that imposes itself uniformly upon all. To show that things weren't as necessary as all that . . . a breach of self-evidence,

DOI: 10.4324/9781003106968-3

of those self-evidences on which our knowledges, acquiescences, and practices rest.

(2000, pp. 226–227)

By grasping the contingency of socio-historical contexts, such ruptures create opportunities for critical self-reflection on the institutions, practices, subject formations, and normative commitments that have led us to constitute ourselves and others as we have (Foucault, 2000).

For this reason, in decolonial work (which emphasizes the subjects and contexts implicated in knowledge production), it is important to state one's own 'locus of enunciation' and 'positionality'. The author is a white female academic who worked in Education Development and was an associate staff member of Sociology in the Humanities Faculty, the University of Cape Town when this research was conducted. Many of the student activists involved in the protests were registered in the programme I convened. I am grateful for the opportunities to interview some of them during and soon after the protests. The data presented here was sourced from interviews and documents by students and staff at UCT, a historically white, research-intensive South African university where the RhodesMustFall protests began in 2015. The data and analysis relate to the humanities because this is where the debates have raged most intensely and because this is where I worked and could access data.

The chapter is structured as follows: First the conceptual framework and method based on the Specialization dimension of Legitimation Code Theory (Maton, 2014) is introduced. I work through each of the three fields of the *epistemic–pedagogic device* or 'EPD' (Maton, 2014) – setting out the data and analysis for each field in turn. But I do not work down the device following the Bernsteinian tradition of a hierarchy of relations from knowledge to curriculum to pedagogy. Instead I show that student activists appropriated decolonial theory to support their cause in the field of pedagogy, against what they experienced as Eurocentric colonial forms of institutional culture, curriculum, and teaching. This case study thus illustrates the recursive nature of the EPD, showing how events in the field of pedagogy have impacted 'upwards' in the field of curriculum development. This is where I move next to analyze contesting sets of academic voices around how to respond to the students' call to 'decolonize the curriculum'. Finally, I draw some conclusions.

Conceptual framework

According to Maton, 'the epistemic – pedagogic device is the focus of domination and resistance, struggle and negotiation, both within education and across wider society' (Maton, 2014, p. 53). He explains how social actors in symbolic fields, such as higher education, compete to control the epistemic–pedagogic device in order to ensure that its measures of achievement and legitimation reflect their own dispositions and practices; 'to control the epistemic–pedagogic device is to control the comparative values of specialization codes and thereby the structuring of a social field' (p. 52). This is a model that can show relations between power, knowledge, and consciousness and how these work between three levels or fields, as shown in Figure 3.1: knowledge production (driven by *epistemic logics*), curriculum design and organization (driven by *recontextualizing logics*), and pedagogy or sites of teaching and learning (driven by *evaluative logics*). Importantly, in Maton's model, each of the fields can shape discourses and practices in the other two fields. So, as noted earlier, I trace how the impetus for change was initiated by students in the pedagogic field, drawing on decolonial theory from the field of knowledge production; and how this in turn led to contestation around policy and practice in the field of curriculum.

In Specialization, Maton identifies two analytically distinct relations that specialize and legitimate knowledge practices in symbolic fields: *epistemic relations* (ER) between a knowledge claim and its object, focus, and methods; and *social relations* (SR) between a knowledge claim and its subject, author, or actor (2014, p. 29). Humanities disciplines are often (though not always) dominated by *knower codes* (ER –, SR+); these are fields where the criteria for achievement, power, and hierarchy lie in the aptitudes and

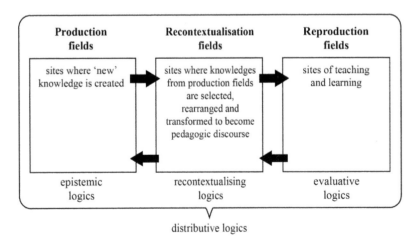

Figure 3.1 The arena created by the epistemic – pedagogic device (EPD) (Maton, 2014, p. 51).

dispositions of the 'right kind of knower' and control over the objects and methods of study are downplayed. In the humanities, hierarchies of knowers, their texts, and theories tend to compete with each other rather than building on one another, with new knowers typically claiming to offer theories that supersede the old (Maton, 2014, p. 92). Consequently, there is fierce contestation around canons and curricula, including the means of debate itself. Only some discourses get selected and recontextualized into curriculum knowledge, privileging the 'gaze' of some knowers over others. Regarding pedagogy, Maton suggests that knower codes progress through strong 'sociality' by building knowers. But privileged gazes in the humanities are acquired tacitly; in order to acquire what 'counts' in a particular field, learners must be socially and culturally positioned to relate to a community of legitimate knowers. Consequently, in the humanities, the distributive logics of unequal societies constrain access to legitimated gazes and to the means of determining their legitimation.

Maton (2014) makes a further distinction between the basis of different kinds of gazes: social attributes of the ideal knower, *subjective relations* (SubR) and ways of interacting with significant others, *interactional relations* (IR). This enables him to identify four gazes (see Figure 3.2) each with a different basis of legitimation.

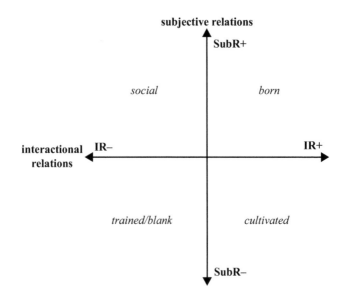

Figure 3.2 The social plane (Maton, 2014, p. 186)

Method

This chapter is based on qualitative data; I captured and selected instances of text from interviews and documents in the public domain that construe particular 'languages of legitimation' and their axiological stances expressed by social actors in the humanities field. From the data I inferred the underlying 'legitimation codes' or organizing principles on which actors base their claims to legitimacy, authority, and specialization. In a third step, I offer my own analysis of 'what's going on here?'. For this I dug deeper into the discursive formations and their associated axiologies in a highly 'raced' post-colonial context to make inferences about how distributive, epistemic, recontextualizing, and evaluative logics might be working to shape actors' stances and claims.

Field of production: a cultivated gaze, decolonial lens

The mere fact that the discourse of the Latin American school of decolonial theory currently resonates strongly with black knowers in the South African academy suggests that 'coloniality' persists in South African higher education institutions, especially in those that are historically white. Decolonial theory is concerned to promote social and epistemic justice; I argue later in the chapter that in South African higher education, there is an ethical obligation to respond to the challenge to decolonize institutional cultures and curricula. Decolonial theory set out to re-frame modern assumptions about epistemology. The Latin American school (Dussel, Mignolo, Escobar, Grosfoguel, Maldonado-Torres) builds on earlier traditions: early anti-colonial thinkers (Cesaire, Ghandi, Senghor, and Du Bois); political-philosophers engaged in anti-colonial national liberation struggles (Nkrumah, Nyere, Cabral, Fanon, and Biko); post-colonial scholars (Said, Hall, Quijano, Chatterjee, Spivak, Chakrabarty, and Bhabha). Here I focus on the writings of just two of the most prominent theorists of Latin American decolonial theory – Enrique Dussel and Walter Mignolo.

In the 1970s Dussel, a philosopher, wrote a historical-materialist re-reading of Western philosophy as a counter-narrative to Hegel's Eurocentric historicism. Starting modern history with the Catholic church's mission in the Americas in the fifteenth century, Dussel critiques Hegel's promotion of Europe as the apex of civilization and his assumption that the rest of the world should follow its path of development (the 'Eurocentric fallacy'). Instead he argues that non-European alterity in the 'periphery' was constitutive of Europe's self-definition as the 'centre'. He launched a scathing critique of the West's 'civilizing mission' (which included education) during and beyond the colonial era, which was used to justify modernity's originary and constitutive violence, 'we do not negate reason (the rationalism of the Enlightenment) but we insist on the irrationality of the violence generated by the myth of modernity' (Dussel, 1993, p. 75). Dussel asserts that modern knowledge claims are implicated in the unjust power relations established by colonialism. His solution is 'transmodernity', defined as the co-realization of an inclusive form of solidarity which European modernity cannot achieve alone (Dussel, 1993).

Following Dussel, two key moves in decolonial theory are first to acknowledge the historical 'epistemicide'[1] of previously colonized knowers and their ways of knowing by the colonizers (Europe and then the West). Second, the decolonial critique announces the end of the 'Oriental' and the 'savage,' that is, the end of the West's self-constitutive 'othering' techniques. Unlike earlier anti-colonial Marxist critiques that framed racism as an ideology used to justify colonialism after the fact (Fanon, 1967), the Latin American decolonial school argue that the racism developed during colonialism continues as 'coloniality' in the present. For example, that the racism of 'coloniality' is used to perpetuate asymmetrical power relations in contemporary developmental policies and programmes (Maldonado-Torres, 2007, pp. 243–244).

A key concept in decolonial theory is that of 'modernity/coloniality' (Mignolo, 2010b; Quijano, 2007) which captures the idea that unjust colonial relations continue into the present both as an effect of the colonial era and contemporaneously as a consequence of the way the West has imposed its version of modernity on the rest of the world. The modern episteme has been institutionalized and universalized through the modern university system, the modern disciplines and through the five hegemonic (ex-colonial) European languages (Grosfoguel, 2013, p. 74).

In LCT terms, decolonial theorists argue that the distributive logic of modernity/coloniality's EPD (who gets access) is entangled with its epistemic logics (the basis of knowledge creation). In this sense they redefine the contexts of production of the modern canons. They argue that because the modern disciplines were generated from within colonial apparatuses and power relations, thus not only the contents of the modern disciplines but also their foundational epistemic assumptions should be interrogated (Escobar, 2002; Grosfoguel, 2008; Mignolo, 2011). Thus, 'epistemic de-colonization' involves exposing 'the hidden complicity between the rhetoric of modernity and the logic of coloniality' (Mignolo, 2005, p. 111). This spatializing and temporalizing of reason's European history leads to the demoting of Western knowledge claims from universal status to just one of many competing social gazes (Mignolo, 2010a).[2]

W. Mignolo (1993) is a semiotician who introduced Foucault's concept of the 'locus of enunciation' into decolonial discourse. He uses this concept to argue that he is not advocating that a subaltern woman is necessarily better placed to understand subaltern women's issues (a social gaze). Instead he proposes that all knowing subjects are inscripted into a network of disciplinary and cultural structures, processes, and places that shape their knowing, and that critical to accounting for the workings of social relations in knower codes, is to understand from where the knower is speaking (this includes the historical formation of the knower's agenda and intended audience):

> Whoever writes in whatever place at whatever time writes within, outside or in the margins of disciplinary configurations and cultural identities. Consequently, the 'true' account of a subject matter in the form of knowledge or understanding will be transacted in the respective communities of interpretation as much for its correspondence to what is taken for 'real' as for the authorizing locus of enunciation constructed in the very act of describing an object or a subject.
>
> (Mignolo, 1993, p. 336)

Mignolo takes both epistemic and social relations into account, offering a more subtle argument than simply promoting an alternative social gaze to that of the Western modern, 'I am concerned with the tension between the inscription of an epistemological subject within a disciplinary context and its inscriptions within a hermeneutic context in which race, gender and tradition compete with the goals, norms and rules of the disciplines' (1993, p. 335). Further, Mignolo's proposal for a 'pluri-dimensional hermeneutic' involves a shift from the 'colonial discourse analysis' (of written texts) to a 'colonial semiosis' that captures the oral, pictorial, and other means of symbolic communication used by, for example, Amerindian cultures.

Analysis

In LCT terms, decolonial theorists articulate the idea that the same distributive logics of the political economy of colonialism (exploitative, extractive, and violent relations) are implicated in the social and symbolic relations of knowledge production between the 'centre' and the 'periphery' in the modern era. In this they have articulated a scathing critique of modern institutionalized knowledge practices from a Southern or colonized perspective, reminding us that the legacy of 'coloniality' gets into not only the social relations of knowledge production, but also the historical contexts of its production and therefore epistemological premises. If one accepts their arguments and re-historicizing of the contexts of production of the modern disciplines, then one's ontological moorings have to shift, certainly for knower codes in the humanities. Further, their work includes a call for social and epistemic justice for previously colonized peoples and thus carries a high axiological charge. This is achieved by a cosmology that sets up the evils of colonialism against the innocence and violation of the colonized (Mbembe, 2001, p. 243).

However, decolonial theorists are silent on the relations internal to knowledge and thus on the differentiated nature of knowledge structures and their implications for knowledge-building and curriculum. This leaves them open to accusations of 'knowledge-blindness'. However, as I have argued earlier, a careful analysis of the subjective and interactional relations proposed by theorists such as Mignolo and Martín Alcoff, plus their advocacy of an inclusive teleology via concepts such as a 'pluriversity' (Walter Mignolo, 2013) and 'transmodernity' (Dussel, 2002), suggests that they do not base their claims on a crude social gaze, nor are they wanting to simply install a new set of knowers and ways of knowing and throw out the old. While advocating a weakening of the classification and framing of knowledge and its production by modern Western institutions, to open it up to previously excluded knowers, their end goal is to enrich humanity's stock of knowledge. This reading of key decolonial theorists suggests they are committed to the 'sociality' of knowledge production and want to open up rather than close down conversations about knowledge.

In terms of LCT (Specialization), decolonial theorists assume that all knowledge forms are *knower codes* and base their own claims on a *cultivated gaze* with a *discursive lens* (SubR −, IR+) (Maton, 2014). However, because they argue for a 'new way of seeing' that includes 'coloniality' as the 'darker side of modernity', I think they would want to flip the script – rather than be defined in terms of LCT concepts (articulated from a modern/Western locus of enunciation), they offer us a new lens altogether – a *cultivated gaze* with a *decolonial lens*. On the basis of this gaze they would undoubtedly want to include LCT in the conversation, but on new terms of engagement that might entail re-negotiating the rules for how the interactional relations of cultivated gazes are conducted, leading to a more inclusive transmodern/pluriversal gaze that accommodates local knowledges.

However, decolonial theorists do not address the fields of curriculum or pedagogy directly. Decolonial theory does not provide principles or conceptual tools for determining what knowledge to select for a 'decolonized curriculum', how it should be taught, or on what basis students should be assessed. While it is tempting for decolonial scholars to continue to engage in theoretical skirmishes in the field of production, it has been left to their followers to take up the theory and interpret its implications for curriculum and pedagogic practice. To trace this, I turn to interpretations of decolonial theory for education practice in my own context, where it was black student activists during the protests of 2015–2017 who put the decolonial agenda firmly on the table as a means of challenging traditional/colonial higher education practices.

Field of pedagogy: a social gaze, psychic lens

While student protests related to fees and readmissions occur regularly on historically black South African campuses, in March 2015 a new spontaneous movement that became known as RhodesMustFall (RMF) erupted at UCT, an elite, historically white campus. The focus of RMF was on removing the statue of arch-imperialist Cecil John Rhodes as a symbol of the racism and whiteness of the institution and the 'black pain' suffered by students. Referring to symbolic as well as economic access, Mbembe notes 'that decolonisation of buildings and public spaces is inseparable from the democratisation of access'; creating the 'conditions that will allow black staff and students to say of the university, "This is my home. I am not an outsider here. I do not have to beg or apologise to be here. I belong here"' (Mbembe, 2016, p. 30).

In October 2015, RMF was superseded by FeesMustFall, a protest against fee increases at the University of the Witwatersrand (Wits) that later included a demand to insource university workers. By the end of 2015, 16 universities and 11 colleges had been shut down by students now demanding 'free decolonized education for all'. In order to force students back to class and protect university property, university managers called poorly trained police and private security forces onto campuses. After two more years of intermittent outbreaks of violence and counter-violence against the protesters, the then-president Jacob Zuma, backed down and promised free education to all students from poor families from 2018.

The data presented here was gathered via interviews with student activists from RMF at UCT and also includes quotes from a book published by a student activist (Chikane, 2018). First, student interviewees expressed a sense of misrecognition and exclusion by the hegemonic white culture at UCT that required them to assimilate to become legitimate knowers:

> Particularly in first year, I swam in self-defeatism, self-doubt, and low self-esteem. 'Black and Stupid' were some of my every day inferences through which I made sense of myself and my abilities.
>
> I was scared my contributions would be viewed as stupid. I feared this would be made concrete by my lack of the proficiency of English, which at the time appeared to be a measure of intelligence.

> Black students feel that their only hope of survival is assimilation.
>
> (Chikane, 2018, p. 64)

> Being at UCT introduced me rather rudely to the lived realities of being black in the white world . . . the public lectures and seminars all seemed to be about lived black realities in South Africa and yet were done by white old men and women.

Second, students shared what the protest movement stood for in their eyes,

> #RhodesMustFall . . . was born on the 9 March 2015 out of pain and frustration, what we later called Black Pain!
>
> By throwing poo at the statue of Rhodes we were showing our disgust with the way Rhodes mistreated our people in the past. Equally, we are showing our disgust at the way UCT celebrates the genocidal Cecil Rhodes. The act of poo-throwing was an institutional critique of UCT.

Third, a few students shared their experiences of the psychological and therapeutic work that went on in 'Azania House' (the administration block occupied by protest movement). One student described how some students were viscerally 'purged' or 'exorcized' as they 'vomited out' the 'white spirits' that possessed them.

> The life of black people is a life of nervous condition. This is true at UCT for all black people. . . . It is this life of nervous condition that drives me and many others either to go mad or commit suicide. . . . We were fearful of what will happen to us while we are in the white world if we are to disrupt white power.
>
> We wanted to get rid of the gaze of white people so that we were free to talk about race with whites out of the room. We needed to separate from whiteness to understand our self-worth – we had to learn how to love ourselves – this was a form of liberation, it was psychic recuperation.
>
> Together we asserted what it means to black and powerful – this felt good, it became addictive. RMF became a form of rehab for sharing experiences of being black at UCT – it was like the AA we were all victims of whiteness – we shared some heart-breaking experiences.

The cry of 'black pain' resonated with most black students on campus who came out in support of the protests. Student leaders used an identity politics based on a racialized polemic to mobilize black students against the enemy of 'whiteness'. By late 2015 the movement became controlled by student activists linked to an Africanist political organization. One interviewee explained that this led to a stronger definition of blackness; not only were whites excluded from the movement, but 'coconuts'[3] and 'other Africans' were no longer welcome.[4] It seems that the movement now required a certain Africanist and/or 'woke' disposition from members of its inner circle.

> Black Consciousness ideas were consolidated in RMF – we were all reacting to white institutional racism. We used a race-based analysis and agreed not to talk about class, ('amandla awethu' was replaced with 'izwe lethu'). We took black South African lived experience as the basis for identity . . . so in the beginning, intersectionality was expressed under a black umbrella.
>
> (Chikane, 2018, p. 56)

While the meme of 'black pain' united black South African students across class, gender, and sexual divisions during the first year of the movement's existence, this was not sustained. As one female interviewee explained, as the Africanist agenda became more dominant, some female and LGBTQI+ members became disgruntled with the patriarchal, authoritarian style of some male leaders. In March 2016, a group of transgender activists expressed their outrage by disrupting the opening and destroying the contents of a photographic exhibition set up to commemorate the founding of the RMF movement. From then onwards it became clear that a political movement based on identity politics was fragmenting; the RMF was absorbed into the broader national campaign for free decolonized education.

The RMF movement's criticism of whiteness at UCT was spelled out in a list of long-term goals. Those relating to knowledge and curriculum included:

> Implement a curriculum which centres Africa and the subaltern. By this we mean treating African discourses as the point of departure – through addressing not only content, but languages and methodologies of education and learning – and only examining western traditions in so far as they are relevant to our own experience.
>
> Introduce a curriculum and research scholarship linked to social justice and the experiences of black people.
>
> (Rhodes Must Fall (RMF) Movement, 2015)

Analysis

The RMF movement adopted a raced social gaze (being positioned as black in South Africa) (SR+, IR –) to legitimate its political message and to unite classed and gendered factions of black students. A raced social gaze is also evident in its proposals for decolonizing the curriculum. The data suggest that over time some groups in the movement shifted to a more essentialist and exclusive born gaze based on a nativist or 'woke' disposition (IR+) as well as a biological or genetic basis for legitimation (SubR+), which later caused the movement to fragment politically. But it must be noted that black students' use of identity politics and a born social gaze originated in a cry of misrecognition. They experienced the hegemonic cultivated gaze of this historically white university as a social gaze based on racialized colonial difference that excluded them as legitimate knowers. In this society where subjectivities remain highly 'raced', it is hardly surprising that students reacted by simply inverting the categories of the colonial gaze to a black social gaze, still based on racialized colonial difference.

Furthermore, there was data to show that some students felt a need to purge themselves of this internalized colonial gaze – described as 'ressentiment' by post-colonial writers such as (Fanon, 2008; Mbembe, 2017; Naicker, 2019).[5] Here we are not dealing with knowledge-building in the formal sense, but with subjects coming to terms with what Fanon identified as the psychic condition of the colonized, which he described as an inferiority complex leading to dependency and self-hatred. For Mbembe (2017) this is a neurosis of victimization based on an internalized, moral inversion of colonial metaphysics. These colonized subjects have to first deal experientially with a psychic condition as a precondition for their self-realization as fully agential knowers. Mbembe (2017) warns that this condition is typically accompanied by a pathological belief that 'authentic' African agency can arise only through the violent destruction of the enemy – an external evil other (Mbembe, 2001, p. 251). LCT does not (yet) cater for this kind of experiential knowing and it is probably inappropriate to label it in LCT terms, but if so pushed, I would name it a 'psychic lens' based on the understandable but deleterious effects of an internalized born/social colonial gaze.

Code clashes in the field of recontextualization

I now turn to the site of curriculum policy and development where I present and analyze stances taken by academics as they debated how to respond to the students' demands. It is noteworthy that it was student action in the field of pedagogy that worked 'up' and not 'down' the EPD to challenge the old recontextualizing rules for curriculum construction. The student protests had a polarizing effect on university staff; they signalled an end to fondly held liberal notions of (white) collegiality and claims to academic freedom as an individual right. In LCT terms, the debate that raged around how to respond to the demand to decolonize the curriculum was a code clash between positions based on social and cultivated gazes. In this section

I discuss three categories of academic voices evident in the data: a traditional academic voice, black radical voices, and an institutional response, each based on a different gaze or lens.

Traditional academic voice, a cultivated gaze: colonial lens

In 2016 a postgraduate student interviewed academics in the humanities faculty about their views on decolonizing their curricula (Baijnath, 2017). She concluded that there was little consensus on what decolonization might mean, while few academics had a strong enough grasp of decolonial theory to attempt substantial curriculum change. One responded, 'I'm not yet sure it's a coherent idea' while another stated, 'I think that the kinds of issues that they raised are things I already teach'. All interviewees talked about the content of their courses; none mentioned social relations, culture, language, or pedagogy. One retorted,

> You remember how in feminism they would say 'add a little gender and stir', and you have your gender perspective? You could also say 'add a little blackness and stir' and then you have your new curriculum.
>
> (Baijnath, 2017, p. 51)

There were some oppositional responses suggesting that these academics were out of touch with black students. Some complained about the introduction of identity politics on campus, how it leads to 'intellectual policing' and inhibits possibilities for change. Others asserted that the students' demands were incompatible with their 'academic freedom' to determine what to teach.

Analysis

Some of the data gathered from traditional academics suggests a lack of awareness of the socio-historical specificity of the curriculum and that it may fail to address the burning issues that their students face. This analysis was supported by the Report of the Ministerial Committee on Transformation and Social Cohesion and the Elimination of Discrimination in Public Higher Education Institutions which described 'the transformation of what is taught and learnt' as 'one of the most difficult challenges this sector is facing'.

> Given the decontextualised approaches to teaching and learning that are evident in virtually every institution, it is recommended that institutions give consideration to the development of curriculum approaches

that sensitise students to the place of, and the issues surrounding South Africa on the African continent and in the world at large.

(Council on Higher Education, 2008, p. 21)

Old taken-for-granted assumptions that the pedagogic norm is a privileged white middle class student works in exclusionary ways for most black students. In the humanities, the problems surrounding assimilationist/exclusionary curriculum and pedagogic practices and a lack of shared contexts and forms of sociality are compounded the implicit nature of the legitimate gaze and the invisibility of its criteria for assessment. What is assumed to be a cultivated gaze (IR+) by those in power – an ostensibly teachable and learnable curriculum – may be experienced as a colonial social gaze (SR+) – as a curriculum accessible only to whites – by cultural 'others'. The protests are a powerful reminder of the consequences of 'knower-blindness' by academics in hegemonic positions and by institutions that arrogantly retain their colonial white settler cultures as the norm.

Black radical academic voice: a social gaze, decolonial lens

During the protests at UCT, senior management set up a working group led by black radical academics outside of regular committee processes, to develop proposals for curriculum change. The Curriculum Change Working Group produced a Curriculum Change Framework (CCF) published in 2018. The CCF emerged from their work with student activists-as-partners in curriculum development at three different sites during the protests. The authors could empathize with the students' 'black pain' and set out to interpret this position for the academic community, stating, 'students are important stakeholders, they must participate in the academic project without having to be stripped from their identities by colonial narratives' (University of Cape Town, 2018, p. 62). The report stressed the urgency of correcting the misrecognition and alienation of black learners, arguing that misrecognized students will be neither motivated nor engaged in their learning. The authors of the CCF were the first to formally articulate a decolonial position – the CCF aims to 'resist deficit and assimilationist models based on Anglonormativity and Eurocentrism' (ibid., p. 58). They understand curriculum change to be about challenging the hierarchies of coloniality,

Central to resisting coloniality is defying colonial authority in what constitutes knowledge, how it is produced and who is allowed to claim custodianship.

(University of Cape Town, 2018, p. 54)

The CCF shifts the terms of curriculum contestation from knowledge to knowers, 'curriculum change at UCT must be black-led' (ibid., p. 54); 'the curriculum must reflect students' cultural capital', and 'bring African ways of knowing to the centre' (ibid., p. 62). It also questioned the legitimacy of the disciplines, 'curriculum change is about contesting power, especially disciplinarity, which carries colonial narratives'. They are in effect calling for a new set of knowers to control the EPD.

Black radical academic voice: a cultivated gaze, decolonial lens

Not all black academics agreed with the CCF. Some interviewees implicitly critiqued it. One asked,

> Does it mean learning only about Black thinkers? . . . is this the only way to approach decolonization? . . . We agree to the need for the politics of representation – but this is not what we consider to be substantive decolonization. . . . We are not going to teach students that 'the West is bad and the rest is good'. We want to interrupt this 'lazy history'. The 'decolonial turn' wants to start anew. This is romantic idealism. . . . Colonialism has reconfigured the world – and we have to live with it and learn about it.

This academic legitimated curriculum knowledge on the basis of a cultivated gaze: decolonial lens.

> We start by insisting that students know what they are critiquing. . . . Students must have a sense of the world from a wide perspective. . . . It's not about having the correct identity or politics, but what you know and how you work with that. . . . We teach that the meanings of concepts are contingent on their historical context – they can't just be lifted from elsewhere – we need to find a vernacular language that can interpret modern political concepts for this context.

Analysis

The authors of the CCF critique the 'whiteness' of UCT's institutional culture and its ossified, 'colonial' curriculum based on supposedly open cultivated gazes (but carrying a colonial optic). In their concern to correct the institution's 'knower-blindness', the CCF emphasizes the misrecognition of knowers in an institutional space experienced as racist and exclusionary but leave themselves open to the accusation of 'knowledge-blindness'. If this analysis is correct, then in LCT terms the claims of the CCF are legitimated by a social gaze with a decolonial lens.

All modern/colonial education systems in the South face the challenge of producing alternative modes of subjectivity and sociality to underpin knowledge-building. The challenge is to work with the 'messy contradictory' problems of the 'post-colonial condition' and imagine what kinds of learning experiences and curricula will free all knowers from colonial racialized subjectivities and essentialized binaries.

Responses to the Curriculum Change Framework (2018): cultivated gazes

Unsurprisingly, the CCF caused heated contestation. A website was set up for staff to respond:

> The CCF is based on a very specific set of social science theories. It fails to take disciplinary differences into account. It can't work for the natural and applied sciences.
>   The CCF's theory of knowledge is reductionist – knowledge and curriculum appear to be equated with power relations (only).
>   The CCF endorses a race-based criterion for who can drive the curriculum.
>
> (University of Cape Town, 2018)

Thereafter, UCT's Senate Teaching and Learning Committee produced a formal, internal document 'Taking Curriculum Change Forward' (Senate Teaching and Learning Committee, 2019) that takes into account the CCF and responses to it. It proposes a set of principles to inform an institutional review of the undergraduate curriculum going forward. The document includes measured critiques of the CCF that aim to correct its 'knowledge-blindness'. For example, it states that the 'radical relativizing of knowledge' by the CCF and its 'emphasis on positionality also entails the potential to silence' (ibid., p. 5). Further that 'students' social identities or lived experiences cannot be the only grounds on which students engage or make knowledge claims' while the 'pedagogic challenge is to help students make sense of the gap between the "powerful knowledge" of the disciplines and their lived experience' (ibid., p. 5). The document defends academic expertise and the specialized nature of knowledge (ibid., p. 10). Finally, it calls for a coordinated, collective, and dialogical approach to curriculum review and reform.

Analysis

Identity politics tends to emerge in political struggles in response to misrecognition. This is surely a healthy form of assertion required to reclaim the agency of subordinated groups. But when transferred to educational fields, a politics of identity works as a social gaze that is insufficiently inclusive to build knowledge and potentially silences voices from other social positions. This concern was taken up by the Senate Teaching and Learning Committee. However, in settler societies like South Africa, it is not helpful to simply dismiss social gazes as reductionist or anti-intellectual. In contexts where socio-cultural distance and lack of intersubjectivity between knowers is an effect of considerable ignorance and arrogance by white people, what is intended as a cultivated gaze by white teaching staff may well be experienced as a social gaze by black students (previously labelled a cultivated gaze: colonial lens). In such cases, the decolonial instinct to open up the classification and framing of knowledge to colonized knowers and their ways of knowing is critical to the knowledge-building project in order to correct blind-spots in hegemonic ways of knowing and give 'others' access to the academy without requiring assimilation. This might permit knowledge production to better address local problems and introduce new concepts and methods to the global stock of knowledge.

The heated contestations around a decolonized curriculum on South African campuses may be symptomatic of a deeper problem related to the undoing of colonial subjectivization and the ongoing challenge to work for alternative forms of subjectification, education, and culture that can free us from gazes based on colonial difference and keep the intellectual conversation open to those with whom we disagree. In this sense Maton's (2014) advocacy for the value of interactional relations over subjective relations is critical. The institutional and epistemic conditions that enable open forms of 'sociality' around knowledge-building in the academy should be valued and protected. At the same time the terms of engagement for knowledge-building conversations in the post-colony need to be re-calibrated by those previously colonized to guarantee their full participation. This includes the challenge raised by the CCF of how to include students as legitimate participants in the curriculum decolonization project. Following Mbembe (2016) and the decolonial theorists discussed earlier, this will mostly likely be realized and legitimated by a pluriversal, cultivated gaze: decolonial lens that adopts a 'horizontal strategy of openness to dialogue among different epistemic traditions' and a 'radical refounding of our ways of thinking that can transcend disciplinary divisions' (ibid., p. 37).

Conclusion

This chapter has demonstrated the value of LCT Specialization for analyzing contesting languages of legitimation around decolonizing the curriculum in the humanities in a post-colonial context – as a code clash between social gazes and cultivated gazes. However, in post-colonial contexts with long histories of violence, exploitation, and racism, I exploited LCT's conceptual flexibility to suggest new lenses to accommodate the data – namely a colonial lens, a decolonial lens, and a psychic lens.

Ironically, it is the much-maligned Western academy that is not only the object of decolonial critique but has provided the political freedom and material and institutional conditions for the development of the critique itself. In this sense, this study confirms Bernstein's insight into the internal contradiction of the pedagogic device, namely that offers new knowers access to 'unthinkable knowledge' which in turn they can use to take control of the device itself. In post-colonial societies where civil society is weak, it is of vital importance that new educated elites not only take control of the pedagogic device, but use it to build civil society.

Acknowledgements

I am grateful to Veeran Naicker, a PhD student funded by the National Institute for the Humanities and Social Sciences who provided insightful comments on a draft and enriched its theoretical resources.

Notes

1 While this may be a correct description for those languages and cultures that were deracinated by colonialism, it is over-stated and unhelpful for the South African and other contexts where indigenous languages have been preserved. There is already important work being done to resurrect the black archive (see for example Kumalo S.H. (2019) 'Khawuleza – an instantiation of the Black Archive').
2 In his study of British cultural studies, Maton (2014) points out that the redescription of a cultivated gaze to a social gaze is a move typical of social gazes. However, he also concedes that 'critiques based on social gazes correct the essentialist temptation to misrecognize a canon as asocial and ahistorical' (2014, p. 101).
3 Coconuts are assimilated blacks who have taken on white middle class culture, often as a result of elite schooling.
4 This trend corresponds to what Achille Mbembe has called 'the new nativism'. On the one hand, it operates on the basis of a form of discursive exclusion that separates 'authentic Africans' as racial insiders from outsiders: the exiled, vulnerable communities and diasporic configurations from other continents. On the other, it fails to recognize the plural cosmopolitanism that characterizes Africa. Rather than focusing on what Africa is, Nativism prescribes a moral discourse on what Africa ought to be (Mbembe, 2001, pp. 2–3)
5 Mbembe (2017) has a more sophisticated analysis than that of Fanon's – the latter written during the first wave of anti-colonialism. Mbembe argues that in the late global capitalist era it is becoming increasingly difficult to distinguish between coloniality and modernity – this idea is contained in his concept 'the becoming black of the world'.

References

Baijnath, M. (2017) *Engaging with transformation of the Humanities curriculum at an English-medium research-intensive South African university: Decolonisation and academic agency in an era of uncertainty* (Masters thesis, University of Cape Town, Cape Town).

Chatterjee, P. (2011) *Lineages of political society: Studies in postcolonial democracy*. New York: Columbia University Press.

Chikane, R. (2018) *Breaking a rainbow, building a nation: The politics behind #MustFall movements*. Johannesburg: Picador Africa.

Council on Higher Education. (2008) *Report of the ministerial committee on transformation and social cohesion and the elimination of discrimination in public higher education institutions*. Retrieved from www.che.ac.za.

Dussel, E. (1993) 'Eurocentrism and modernity (Introduction to the Frankfurt Lectures)', *Boundary, 20*(3), 65–76.

Dussel, E. (2002) 'World systems and "trans"-modernity', *Nepantla, 3*(1), 221–244.

Escobar, A. (2002) *Worlds and knowledges otherwise: The Latin American modernity/coloniality*. Paper presented at the Tercer Congreso Internacional de Latin Americanistas en Europa, Amsterdam.

Fanon, F. (1967) *Political essays: Racism and culture, in/ towards the African Revolution* (Trans. by H. Chevalier). New York: Grove Press.

Fanon, F. (2008) *Black skins, white masks* (Trans. by C. L. Markmann). London: Pluto Press.

Foucault, M. (2000) *Essential Works of Michel Foucault 1954–1984*. Vol. 3. London and New York: Penguin Books.

Grosfoguel, R. (2008) 'Developmentalism, modernity, and dependency theory in Latin America'. In W. Mignolo, I. Silverblatt and S. Saldívar-Hull (Eds.), *Coloniality at large: Latin America and the postcolonial debate* (pp. 307–347). Durham, NC: Duke University Press.

Grosfoguel, R. (2013) 'The structure of knowledge in Westernized universities: Epistemic racism/sexism and the four genocides of the long 16th Century', *Human Architecture: Journal of the Sociology of Self-Knowledge, 11*(1), 73–90.

Maldonado-Torres, N. (2007) 'On the coloniality of being: Contributions to the development of a concept', *Cultural Studies, 21*(2–3), 240–270.

Maton, K. (2014) *Knowledge and knowers: Towards a realist sociology of education*. London: Routledge.

Mbembe, A. (2001) *On the post-colony*. Berkeley: University of California Press.

Mbembe, A. (2016) 'Decolonizing the university: New directions', *Arts and Humanities in Higher Education, 15*(1), 29–45.

Mbembe, A. (2017) *Critique of black reason* (Trans. by L. Dubois). Durham, NC: Duke University Press.

Mignolo, W. (1993) 'Colonial and postcolonial discourse: Cultural critique or academic colonialism?' *Latin American Research Review, 28*(3), 120–134.

Mignolo, W. (2005) '*Prophets facing sidewise*: The geopolitics of knowledge and the colonial difference', *Social Epistemology, 19*(1), 111–127.

Mignolo, W. (2010a) 'Delinking: The rhetoric of modernity, the logic of coloniality and the grammar of de-coloniality'. In W. Mignolo and A. Escobar (Eds.), *Globalisation and the decolonial option* (pp. 449–514). London: Routledge.

Mignolo, W. (2010b) 'Introduction: Coloniality of power and de-colonial thinking'. In W. Mignolo and A. Escobar (Eds.), *Globalization and the decolonial option* (pp. 1–21). London: Routledge.

Mignolo, W. (2011) 'Epistemic disobedience and the decolonial option', *Transmodernity: Journal of Peripheral Cultural Production of the Luso-Hispanic World*, *1*(2), 44–66.

Mignolo, W. (2013) 'Geopolitics of sensing and knowing: On (de)coloniality, border thinking, and epistemic disobedience', *Confero: Essays on Education, Philosophy and Politics*, *1*(1), 129–150.

Naicker, V. (2019) 'Ressentiment in the postcolony', *Angelaki*, *24*(2), 61–77. Retrieved from DOI: 10.1080/0969725X.2019.1574079

Quijano, A. (2007) 'Coloniality and modernity/rationality', *Cultural Studies*, *21*(2–3), 168–178.

Rhodes Must Fall (RMF) Movement. (2015) 'UCT Rhodes Must Fall Mission Statement', *The Salon*, *9*, 6–8.

Senate Teaching and Learning Committee. (2019) *Taking curriculum change forward*. Cape Town: UCT.

University of Cape Town. (2018) *Curriculum change framework*. Cape Town: UCT.

4 Decolonising the university

Some thoughts on recontextualising knowledge

Mlamuli Nkosingphile Hlatshwayo

Introduction

The university in the Global South is under intense critique for its lack of transformation and the snail's pace of decolonisation (Heleta, 2018; Hlatshwayo and Fomunyam, 2019; Ndlovu-Gatsheni, 2013a). The academy has been accused of resisting transformation by undertaking various processes of 'reform', 'change' and 'adjustment' designed to give the sense that transformation is being enacted – yet which allow its structures of power to remain intact (Hlatshwayo and Shawa, 2020). Underpinning this critique is the assumption that universities continue to produce and reinforce the epistemic and cognitive violence of the colonial project (Kamanzi, 2016; Keet, 2014; Kumalo, 2018). This phenomenon of the university reinscribing structures of power is not peculiar to South Africa, but is often accompanied by protest as groups within the academy attempt to push back.

The irony of using the works of British, French and British-Australian theorists, Bernstein, Bourdieu and Maton, to explicate the ways in which battles for the curriculum occur in a bid for decoloniality is not lost on me. But my project is not to reject or overthrow all that can be in some way linked to the Global North. Indeed this would be futile in a globalised world, as I will argue later. Rather I want to make sense of how the epistemic traditions so long undermined and absent can take up their rightful place and move us forwards and I believe that Legitimation Code Theory (LCT) offers a set of useful insights for this endeavour.

In particular LCT counters the knowledge-blindness of much of the sociology of education (including many of the calls for decolonisation). Knowledge-blindness entails rightly understanding intellectual developments in the academy and beyond as emerging from issues of social power and institutional politics but then being blind to the extent to which the knowledge practices in turn shape social power and institutional politics. Furthermore, knowledge-blindness leads to research which treats all knowledge

DOI: 10.4324/9781003106968-4

as generic with no recognition about how different fields construct different forms of knowledge to different ends. Understanding the struggles being fought over knowledge and education requires a deep understanding of the differentiated and specialised contexts and practices of each field. 'Knowledge is socially produced by means of antecedent knowledge and how this is done forms the specific (though not monopolistic) concern of intellectual fields' (Maton, 2014, p. 44). The *epistemic–pedagogic device* (Maton, 2014) allows us to engage with deliberations about how and where symbolic control is created, maintained, transformed and changed in society.

The Epistemic–Pedagogic Device (EPD)

The late British sociologist Basil Bernstein (2000) introduced what he called the 'pedagogic device' to trace the different fields by which knowledge is made and transmitted in educational practice. For Bernstein, the pedagogic device comprised three different yet internally related fields of practice: the field of production (the site where new knowledge is developed, such as the laboratory, and disseminated through conferences, journal articles and academic books), the field of recontextualisation (the site of curriculum design, where decisions are made as to which fields of production to draw from, and which issues from the field of production should be selected for inclusion, and how these should be organised, and articulated through syllabus documents, course guides and textbooks), and the field of reproduction (the site of teaching and learning, including assessment practices, where forms of the recontextualised knowledge are presented to students for their engagement). Building on this work, Karl Maton (2014) developed the 'epistemic–pedagogic device' (hereafter the EPD) to argue that the fields are not only interrelated but also dialectical. In other words, knowledge does not always or only move from the field of production to the field of reproduction via the field of recontextualisation. New knowledge could move dialectically from the field of reproduction to the field of production, with an agent drawing on their own teaching and learning experiences to contribute to intellectual knowledge-building.

In this chapter, I focus on the recontextualisation field, where the curriculum is constructed. The overarching distributive logics at play across the EPD regulate access to both principled and everyday meanings and then the recontextualising logics at play in the recontextualising field regulate the de-location and pedagogising of knowledge.

Bernstein (1975) suggests that the process of recontextualisation is largely governed by two sets of rules (or logics), which he terms, instructional discourse (ID) and regulative discourse (RD). Instructional discourse focuses on the selection, sequencing, pacing and assessment of pedagogic

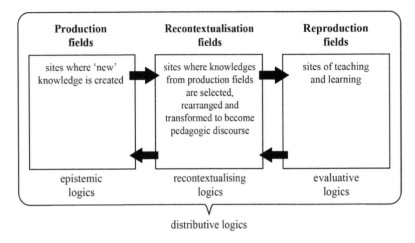

Figure 4.1 The arena created by the epistemic–pedagogic device (EPD) (Maton, 2014, p. 51).

practices. Regulative discourse focuses on the implicit, hidden and assumed morals, ethics and values that shape and influence curriculum design decisions. Academics and curriculum designers, whom Bernstein refers to as recontextualising agents, infuse their own agendas, ideologies and beliefs into the curricula they create (Boughey and McKenna, 2021). This constitutes what Apple (1971) calls the 'hidden curriculum', that is, our taken-for-granted ideologies that we impose on our curricula. In decolonial terms, this could be seen as the site where coloniality most explicitly manifests, in that challenging Western epistemic traditions and calling for the re-centring of African and Global South knowledges and perspectives is seen as contesting 'truth', encapsulated in a 'traditional' and 'well-established' canon. Gordon (2015) and to some extent, Kumalo (2020) challenge organised disciplinarity and the entrenchment of the canon, and propose alternative inter/trans/cross-disciplinaries that draw on different epistemologies from Africa and the Global South in our curriculum imaginations.

While the EPD offers us a 'clean' analytical framework with which to see knowledge being pedagogised across the three different fields, a commitment to decoloniality demands that I recognise the fallibility of this framework if taken literally rather than heuristically. In making sense of the practical struggles for transformation and decolonisation, I argue that they cannot be classified and categorised as belonging in one field only. Struggles for decolonisation in general and recontextualising knowledge in particular tend to be 'messy', complex, dialectical, intersectional and often transcend narrow fields of practice in calling to our attention the need to move beyond formalised disciplines, canons and fields. As Maton (2014, p. 52) indicates, 'actors struggle over control of the arena as a whole, relations between fields, and relations within fields'.

In this chapter, I use the EPD in general and the field of recontextualisation in particular to bring to light the dialectical struggles that are occurring in South African higher education. This offers a useful set of concepts not only to reveal these struggles, but also to open up opportunities to make necessary decolonial interventions, by interrelating power, knowledge and consciousness. Understanding the EPD is thus useful for exploring colonial domination and control because it allows us to see how power relations are translated into educational practices and how educational practices can be translated into power relations.

I have divided this chapter into two parts. In Part I, I focus on explicating our understanding of coloniality/decoloniality. In Part II, I apply the EPD through our discussion of the emergent calls for transformation in the South African academy. I then move to the heart of the chapter: providing an argument for why I believe a focus on the struggles for knowledge is central to decolonisation and transformation.

Part I
Conceptualising coloniality and decoloniality

Decolonial scholars propose the terms 'coloniality' and 'decoloniality' to make sense of the enduring patterns of colonial contact and institutionalised entrenchment of the values of the historically colonised world, including in our universities, curricula, teaching practices and knowledge production (Grosfoguel, 2007; Maldonado-Torres, 2007; Ndlovu-Gatsheni, 2013b). The notion of the distributive logic of the EPD allows us to understand the ways in which coloniality marks who is to be a legitimate knower and who is not, and who is entitled to distribute knowledge; furthermore this logic conditions who may claim what and under which conditions, and thereby sets the limits of what constitutes legitimate discourse. This can be seen to manifest as three dialectical yet interrelated struggles – the 'coloniality of power', the 'coloniality of knowledge' and the 'coloniality of being' (Maldonado-Torres, 2016).

The *coloniality of power* focuses on the social, economic, cultural and political inequalities, reproduction and imbalances that continue beyond the formal colonisation and military occupation by the Global North of the Global South. Rodney (1973) in his seminal work entitled 'How Europe Underdeveloped Africa', writes about how Europe structurally engineered underdevelopment in Africa through the extractive, anthropological and colonial nature of African economic development in aiding and supporting Western industrial development. Adopting classical Marxist lenses, Wolpe (1972) provides an alternative conception of this coloniality of power in looking at the apartheid regime in South Africa, where the capitalist class struggled to meet the demand for expanding cheap labour for the industrial economy. This coloniality of power speaks to what Mignolo (2011) refers to as the 'darker side of western modernity', that is, the operational logic whereby concepts of 'universal' Western modernity and scientific progress were accompanied by the colonial project that sought to 'civilise' and 're-educate' the African subjects who were seen as useful labour for the colonial regime. For Césaire (1955) and Said (1978), and more recently Gordon (2011) and Almeida and Kumalo (2018), the colonial project was inherently an existentialist project committed to the 'thingi-fication' of the colonised subalterns, denying humanity, culture(s), spirituality, knowledges and modes of being in the attempt to socially re-construct the colonised into useful colonial subjects or 'things'. Said (1978) writes about the ontological and epistemic death of the oriental *Other*. This goes far beyond excluding people who are not deemed to be legitimate knowers within the distributive logic of the EPD because these knowers are reimagined in the colonial mind as not human, but as a colonial tool and object, needing to be owned, controlled and dominated.

The *coloniality of knowledge* refers to the continuing systemic and institutionalised influence of colonisation through knowledge production, the academy, curriculum design and teaching and learning practices that decontextualise learners and which remain dominant in the university (Hlatshwayo and Fomunyam, 2019; Khunou *et al.*, 2019; Kumalo, 2018; Boughey and McKenna, 2021). At the heart of the distributive logic of coloniality is Kant's notion of *cogito, ergo sum*, which constitutes a central organising myth of the Western philosophical conception of logic, rationality and reason (Hlatshwayo and Shawa, 2020; Hlatshwayo *et al.*, 2020; Le Grange, 2019). The 'I' in this Western epistemic tradition is the colonising European subject who refuses to recognise and acknowledge different beings, knowledges and epistemic traditions outside of the domain of Euro-American thought. Rejecting the Cartesian duality between the individual and society, between the rational and the affective, between body and mind, and between human and nature is central to the call for decoloniality.

The *coloniality of being* refers to the ways that universities in general, and historically white universities in particular, are structurally involved in the social reproduction of 'natives of nowhere' who are dislocated from their being, indigenous epistemic traditions, identity and cultural belonging (Kumalo, 2018; Buntin, 2006). Kumalo employs the story of the late apartheid journalist, Nat Nakasa, who committed suicide by jumping out of a building in New York after banishment by the apartheid regime, to explicate the assimilationist challenges that students have to navigate when accessing historically white universities (see also Alasow, 2015; Naicker, 2016; Open Stellenbosch Collective, 2015). Kumalo (2018) agrees with Ndlovu-Gatsheni (2018a) in his suggestion that this coloniality of being presents itself through the ontological (and existential) exiling of the colonised from themselves, their languages, identities, names, spaces, time and socio-spirituality.

The coloniality of power, coloniality of being and coloniality of knowledge are, in our view, central to the distributive logics of the academy. The 2015–2016 student protests organised under the banners of #RhodesMustFall and #FeesMustFall re-centred ongoing calls to re-configure the university and reimagine access, curriculum, pedagogy and the broader institutional culture(s) Carolissen & Kiguwa (2018); Cornell and Kessi, 2017). I now turn to the possibilities that the EPD offers in exploring the field of recontextualisation, where knowledge is selected, sequenced and articulated in curriculum documents.

Part II
A brief context on the struggles for decolonising the university

Contemporary transformation struggles in South African higher education have often foregrounded three key aspects that attempt to respond to the calls for transformation and decolonising the university. These are: the purposes of the university; curriculum design and its potential imaginations; and teaching and learning (Booysen, 2016; Khunou *et al.*, 2019; Mbembe, 2016). One of the significant contributions of the #RhodesMustFall and #FeesMustFall movements was to force us to reflect on our understanding of what constitutes the public university in South Africa (see Hlatshwayo and Shawa, 2020; Mbembe, 2016; Ndlovu-Gatsheni, 2013a). A common understanding is that the current university in its constitution and formulations functions at least in part as a neoliberal teaching machine (Spivak, 2012). It 'economises' activities, processes and people and disregards that which cannot be counted and its efficiency counted (Boughey and McKenna, 2021). In doing this the university disregards its context and seeks to replicate its Euromodern counterparts in North America and Western Europe. For Mbembe (2016), Kumalo (2018) and Heleta (2016), universities in South Africa value and legitimate curricula and syllabi rooted in a colonial and apartheid logic constructed under the guise of neoliberal strategic reforms. The distributive logics of colonialism have been transmogrified into the distributive logics of neoliberalism.

There are at least two critiques of the current calls for decolonisation of the university. The first argues that the public university is a neoliberal, colonising institution that needs to be entirely dismantled so that in its place a multiversity, or alternatively a pluriversity, can emerge (Mbembe, 2016; Ndlovu-Gatsheni, 2013a, 2018b). The operational logic is that this pluriversity or multiversity will embrace different epistemic traditions and begin to look at the world from the perspective of Africa and the Global South.

The second critique, largely advanced by Jansen (2017), Habib (2019), and more recently, Teferra (2020), suggest impending doom for the current university in South Africa as a result of a decline of standards that come with the move towards decolonisation. This decline of the 'South African university' is driven, at least according to Jansen (2017), by the pressures brought by the 2015–2016 student protests which have challenged the entire repertoire of the EPD and its current distributive logics, including curricula, teaching and learning and institutional cultures, and language in all public universities.

It should be highlighted that central to the recontextualising logic is the reproduction of the coloniality of knowledge through language, with various scholars building on the work of Wa Thiong'o (1986) and Asante (1991) to critique the hegemonic role of the English language. This goes far beyond concerns about the pedagogical challenges brought about through learning in an additional language to the consideration of the discursive limits in making sense of and unpacking indigenous knowledge systems and the nuanced lifeworlds of Africans. For Quijano (2007), Ndlovu-Gatsheni (2018b) and Hlatshwayo (2019b), this becomes an opportunity to engage in 'epistemic disobedience' in moving beyond and 'de-linking' from Western epistemic traditions and beginning to re-centre other *Othered* epistemic traditions that enable, facilitate and reinforce us – our ontological and epistemic lives – in all our complexities and diversities.

Recently, Le Grange (2019) and Hlatshwayo and Shawa (2020) have built on the work of Pinar (1975) to re-construct the term *ubuntu currere* (Ubuntu curriculum) to advance a democratic and social justice conception of the academy, where organised curriculum is not *a priori* and rather builds upon student experiences in the university. This concept of curriculum constitutes the rejection of the top-down, hierarchical power relations in curriculum design and calls for an attempt at flattening this curriculum hierarchy through inclusion, diversity and democratic thought in such curriculum spaces. Such challenges to the existing recontextualising logics will need to take very different forms in different fields. In fields with stronger social relations, where being a particular kind of knower is central to success, as is common across the humanities, there may be more cracks to leverage towards recognising the wealth of knowledge(s) long excluded from the academy. In fields with what LCT (Maton, 2014) terms stronger epistemic relations, on the other hand, such as many fields in the natural sciences, where there is general consensus about the nature of knowledge deemed legitimate and this knowledge is strongly bounded, the process of challenging well-established practices may be particularly challenging, and even the idea that there is always an ideal knower may be contested. The colonial project is strongly evident across the academy but the colonialities of power, knowledge and being manifest in varied ways across disciplinary contexts and attempts to shift the distributive logics of the academy will need to take this into account.

Furthermore, the distributive logics of the academy do not contain themselves only to the formal curriculum. Various institutional mechanisms and structures, such as the hegemonic institutional culture(s), space and spatial justice, university practices and ceremonies, buildings and statues are experienced by many Black students as daily reminders that they are not recognised by and do not belong in the academy (Hlatshwayo, 2015; Mahabeer *et al.*, 2018). Black academics have had to negotiate institutional racism, sexism, harassment, discrimination and epistemic violence in being forced to prove their legitimacy, competence and belonging (Booi *et al.*, 2017; Mahabeer *et al.*, 2018; Nzimande, 2017). Khoza-Shangase (2019), for example, diagnoses herself as suffering from intellectual and emotional toxicity in grappling with the institutional racism and white privilege at a research intensive university, which led to her own depression.

Black working class students who are the first in their family to come to university are especially side-lined by the recontextualising logics of the curriculum (Hlatshwayo, 2015; Vincent and Hlatshwayo, 2018). Epistemic marginality is particularly confronting in historically white universities as they tend to attract, train and retain Black academics from middle class backgrounds who more likely conform to the dominant institutional culture, and thereby leave the distributive logics unchallenged.

This allows these universities to achieve two things. First, they are able to claim, through affirmative action classifications, that their institution and its departments are demographically transforming in light of the post-apartheid democratic order's rainbow nation logic. Second, these universities are able to maintain their dominant distributive logics without being challenged or forced to reconsider or dismantle them. Hlengwa (2019) and Booi (2015) write about this phenomenon in the emergence of the 'grow your own timber' discourse evidenced in various accelerated development programmes in higher education. Hlengwa (2019) refers to this modus operandi as the university employing 'safe bets', that is, employing Black academics who meet affirmative action categories but who subscribe to and reinforce the distributive logics at play. In this way, the curriculum may have small changes made towards decoloniality but the underpinning recontextualising logic remains unscathed.

In the growing calls for decolonising the curriculum, there appear at least two recontextualising logics jostling for power. These are the 'dismantling' approach to decolonisation, and the 're-centring' approach. The 'dismantling' approach entails not only challenging the recontextualising logic of the curricula and its attendant instructional and regulative discourses, but rejecting Western epistemologies as inherently colonial and racist; and thus as having no theoretical or philosophical value for us to consider (Kamwendo, 2016; Msila and Gumbo, 2016; Samuel, 2017). Madlingozi (2016), advocating for dismantling the conception of transformation and decolonisation, cautions us that we need to resort to the 'cosmogenic' approach in our pursuit of indigenous knowledge.

In the other approach, advocated by Ndlovu-Gatsheni (2018b), Le Grange (2019) and Mbembe (2015), the struggles for the distributive logics of the academy could take a 're-centring' approach, which would be seen in the foregrounding of African and Global South epistemic traditions in the curriculum in that the word is read and understood from the position of Africa first and the world second. This can be seen in how knowledges from Latin America, the Caribbean nations, North America, India, Brazil, and Aotearoa, for example, offer phenomenological and epistemic lenses that help us make sense of coloniality and its different contextual manifestations evidenced through power, capital, labour, knowledge, inequality, oppression and so on. Although I am troubled by the monolithic conception of 'Africa' often suggested by the dismantling approach to transforming the university, I nonetheless support the argument that African epistemic traditions in all their diversity and complexity need to occupy greater significance in curriculum formulations, institutional practices and other important sites of the academy. For Fanon (1963), Makgoba (1997), Madlingozi (2018) and Kumalo (2020), the Black archive is a crucial reference point in reclaiming ourselves, our identities and ways of being in the world, in accounting for the mis-interpretation of African and Global South epistemic traditions, and re-interpreting them in ways that are authentic, true and complex.

I believe that this will take a variety of forms and will require a complex project of making the distributive logics far more explicit and demonstrating the power of recontextualising in ways that challenge the current hegemonies inherent in the curriculum.

Having outlined the emerging struggles for decolonising the university, I argue that largely missing in these debates and emerging literature is the focus on the politics and challenges of recontextualising this knowledge in the academy within a decolonial worldview (Hlatshwayo, 2019a). That is, the ideologies, views, beliefs and values that inform what knowledges academics select and construct in their curricula.

Recontextualising (decolonial) knowledge in the South African academy

Recontextualising decolonial and Afrocentric knowledge could be seen as the central core of the mobilisation efforts of the student movements in 2015–2016 (Alasow , 2015; Bosch, 2017; Ngcobozi, 2015). Many students and progressive academics argue that the political economy of the curriculum, that is, the curriculum in all its facets and complexities, is central to the operations of the academy as a neoliberal colonial entity that continues to perpetuate epistemic, social and cognitive injustices (Hlatshwayo and Fomunyam, 2019; Jagarnath, 2015; Kamanzi, 2016). Largely influenced by new materialism as a philosophical discourse (see Vincent, 2018), these researchers have looked at the ways in which curriculum, institutional culture, physical architecture, spatial justice, and pedagogic practices are all dialectically aligned through the distributive logics to marginalise Black beings (Mbembe, 2015). Decolonising the curriculum is an inherently existential and structural process that includes considering what is being taught, who is teaching, what power relations are embedded in the curriculum, and the often-unequal power relationships between students and academics. It requires that all the spaces in which ideology is at play in the curriculum are opened for critique.

For Kamanzi, the colonial operational architecture reproduces itself in curriculum through reinforcing power, hierarchy, domination and submission in ensuring that academic relations are underpinned by boundaries around who is deemed to be a legitimate knower, and who is deemed to be an illegitimate empty vessel in need of 'training' and 'education'. For Heleta (2018), Mbembe (2016), and Gordon (2007), these boundaries are enforced through the teaching of a deeply troubling and colonising canon that seeks to project itself 1) as the only 'epistemic game in town', 2) that continues to Other and disregard alternative epistemic traditions as without reason, and 3) that perpetuates and maintains the fallacy of the Cartesian duality in its obsession with separating the knower from knowledge itself. The relationship between the self, knowing and the world is intersectional in the Global South, with the mind/body/spirit/soul as all constituting the metaphysical being who is not only located in the world, but has ties with the ancestral realm as well (Ramose, 2015; Tamale, 2020). The 2015–2016 #RhodesMustFall movement, the Black Student Movement and the #Open-StellenboschCollective have focused on, first, re-establishing the consensus that the academy in South Africa is still largely alienating, colonial and needs to be transformed and decolonised. Second, the regulative discourse is shaped by the logics of social justice, which in turn shapes particular kinds of pedagogic practices through the logics of the instructional discourse. This manifests variously through calls for removing the 'dead white men' from the curriculum (Pett, 2015), and in so doing to epistemically 'disobey' the white 'fathers' and 'founders' of modern thought (Hlatshwayo, 2019b). Responding to this challenge, Kumalo (2020) proposes that instead we need to 'resuscitate' and focus on the Black Archive in foregrounding the African epistemic traditions, not to read them and engage them in isolationist and reductionist terms, but rather to relate and compare them with other epistemic traditions in the world. For those in the South African 'teaching machine' (Spivak, 2012), important, seminal works such as writings by Sol Plaatjie, Archie Mafeje, AC Jordan, SEK Mqhayi, Lewis Nkosi, Sylvia Tamale, Percy Mabogo More, Omolara Ogundipe-Lesli, Catherine Obianuju Acholonu and others, still remain largely marginalised within the canon; thus they need to be re-centred in curriculum and engaged with as critical texts in teaching and learning.

Building on the need to return to the Black Archive for critical theoretical resources, Matthews (2018) argues that we need to explicate the 'colonial library' and its recontextualising logics in Political Studies so as to expose students to epistemologies that do not prioritise Euromodernity. When Matthews teaches African Politics, she prescribes dominant Western texts alongside alternative literature that questions the dominant assumptions around 'failed' African states, and in the teaching and learning process, she presents counter hegemonic perspectives on the challenges that continue to confront the continent. This enables students to think critically about the role of authoritative texts in the academy and the need to critique the embedded assumptions that tend to carry that canon. Matthews concedes that merely prescribing the dominant texts next to the 'hegemonic' or seminal ones does not necessarily result in a disruptive or decolonial moment, and that more work still needs to be done in ensuring that the recontextualised literature achieves decolonial aims. Building on the work of Matthews (2018), Kumalo (2018) and Hlatshwayo (2019b) have previously called for the re-centring of African philosophy in the broader recontextualisation of political studies knowledge. Ethnophilosophy, Sage philosophy and the Nationalist-liberation philosophy have rich epistemic resources that enable us to think through philosophy, political theory and Africa beyond the restrictive boundaries of the colonial gaze.

It should be noted that academic freedom and the right to choose the kind of curriculum materials to design and prescribe is a crucial component of the field of recontextualisation and the discursive politics involved (McKenna and Quinn, 2012; McKenna and Boughey, 2014). Academic identity, disciplinary communities, the right to choose which material to include and to exclude, and how (and to what extent) academics can enact teaching and learning practices without undue imposition constitute the very hallmark of the academy. While scholars such as Coetzee (2016), Nongxa (2020) and Sultana (2018) are deeply concerned about what they see as the erosion of academic freedom and the plurality of voices in the academy, I wish to make two arguments in relation to academic freedom and the possibilities for recontextualising decolonial knowledge in the academy.

First, to what extent is true and meaningful decolonisation possible within the confines of institutional autonomy and academic freedom? Simply put, should decolonisation and the ethics of transformation be an institutional choice? Can transformation occur within a neoliberal democratic framework that governs and shapes university management and its policies? Is there any alternative philosophical framework that could be implemented in cultivating a decolonial methodology in curriculum? The answers to these and other questions have an impact on academic freedom and to what extent academics could be incentivised or compelled to recontextualise decolonial knowledge in their curricula. Where such processes are enforced, they can rapidly become a compliance exercise, such as we now see in the inclusion of 'decolonisation' as a line item on curriculum templates at Unisa, the biggest university in South Africa.

Second, curriculum decisions tend to reflect and mirror individual academics' scholarly identities and how they see themselves and their work in relation to their field of research and practice. Hanson (2009), Henkel (2000), and Becher and Trowler (2001) write about how academic identities tend to be shaped and influenced by three key aspects: the discipline, the institution, and a sense of professional affiliation, with Hanson (2009, p. 554) suggesting that 'academics have far greater allegiance to their discipline, a community that extends beyond organizational and national boundaries, than to their employing university'. Although traditional collegiality to an academic culture is generally seen as being on the decline, Trowler (2020) indicates that there is still an affinity to the academy in how academics choose to retain a measure of control over their work. This is perhaps best captured by the academic quoted here, who draws on her field of practice to inform her identity and what she chooses to teach:

> The choices of it, I think as Toni Morrison shows us, language is political, how you frame one's course. . . . I like that even if I disagree with the heart of the argument I use the very provocative idea of New Wars to enter the debate and it is good it is a white woman who provokes that debate and there has been a lot of intellectual responses to that. She is theorizing war and it forces a student to think in different ways; I sure

hope so. *I can't separate my identity. My African feminism is highly framed by my African reality so it is allowed intellectual devotion to thinking about this place, this continent in serious ways, women's work and women's ways of thinking are fundamental to that.*

(interview, from Hlatshwayo, 2019a, p. 99; emphasis added)

In terms of the recontextualising logic, academic freedom and academic identities have material implications for the kinds of knowledge that is recontextualised in curriculum. Both the regulative and instructional discourses underpinning the recontextualising logic are largely shaped by the concepts of academic freedom and the personal and institutional autonomy that academics enjoy in selecting, sequencing and pacing the curriculum for their different course offerings. The promotion of decolonial knowledge as fundamental to the recontextualising logic will need to grapple with the challenges that academic freedom brings, as well the individual identities that academics have, alongside the nature of the target knowledge.

In lieu of a conclusion

In this chapter, I have attempted to provide preliminary thoughts on recontextualising decolonial knowledge into curricula within the South African academy. Through the use of the EPD, I have attempted to theorise and explicate the struggles that are currently taking place in South African higher education. I suggest that foregrounding the recontextualisation of decolonial knowledge should be seen as an epistemic prerequisite to engaging with the critical issues of academic freedom, academic identities, and the constraints on achieving decolonial aims within a neoliberal university.

References

Alasow, J. G. (2015) 'What about "Rhodes (University) must fall"?', *Daily Maverick*, 23 March 2015. Retrieved from www.dailymaverick.co.za/opinionista/2015-03-23-what-about-rhodes-university-must-fall/

Almeida, S. and Kumalo, S. H. (2018) '(De) coloniality through indigeneity: Deconstructing calls to decolonise in the South African and Canadian university contexts', *Education as Change, 22*(1), 1–24.

Apple, M. W. (1971) 'The hidden curriculum and the nature of conflict', *Interchange, 2*(4), 27–40.

Asante, M. K. (1991) 'The Afrocentric idea in education', *The Journal of Negro Education, 60*(2), 170–180.

Becher, T. and Trowler, P. (2001) *Academic tribes and territories: Intellectual enquiry and the cultures of disciplines.* 2nd ed. Buckingham: Society for Research into Higher Education and Open University Press.

Bernstein, B. (1975) 'Class and pedagogies: Visible and invisible', *Educational Studies*, *1*(1), 23–41.

Bernstein, B. (2000) *Pedagogy, symbolic control, and identity: Theory, research, critique.* Revised edition. London: Rowman and Littlefield.

Booi, M. (2015) *Accelerated development programmes for Black academics: Interrupting or reproducing social and cultural dominance* (Master's thesis, Rhodes University, Makhanda, South Africa). Retrieved from http://hdl.handle.net/10962/3338.

Booi, M., Vincent, L. and Liccardo, S. (2017) 'Counting on demographic equity to transform institutional cultures at historically white South African universities?', *Higher Education Research and Development*, *36*(3), 498–510.

Booysen, S. (2016) *Fees must fall.* Johannesburg: Wits University Press.

Bosch, T. (2017) 'Twitter activism and youth in South Africa: The case of# Rhodes-MustFall', *Information, Communication and Society, 20*(2), 221–232.

Boughey, C. and McKenna, S. (2021) *Understanding higher education: Alternative perspectives.* Cape Town: African Minds.

Bunting, I. (2006) 'The higher education landscape under apartheid'. In N. Cloete, P. Maassen, R. Fehnel, T. Moja, T. Gibbon and H. Perold (Eds.), *Transformation in higher education. Global pressures and local realities* (pp. 35–52). The Netherlands: Springer.

Carolissen, R. and Kiguwa, P. (2018) 'Narrative explorations of the micro-politics of students' citizenship, belonging and alienation at South African universities', *South African Journal of Higher Education, 32*(3), 1–11.

Césaire, A. (1955) 'Discourse on colonialism', *Postcolonialisms: An Anthology of Cultural Theory and Criticism*, 60–64.

Coetzee, C. (2016) 'Academic freedom in contexts', *Arts and Humanities in Higher Education, 15*(2), 200–208.

Cornell, J. and Kessi, S. (2017) 'Black students' experiences of transformation at a previously 'white only' South African university: A photovoice study', *Ethnic and Racial Studies, 40*(11), 1882–1899.

Fanon, F. (1963) *The wretched of the earth.* London: Penguin Books.

Gordon, L. R. (2007) 'Problematic people and epistemic decolonization: Toward the postcolonial in Africana political thought'. In N. Persram (Ed.), *Postcolonialism and political theory* (pp. 121–142). Lanham, MD: Lexington Books.

Gordon, L. R. (2011) 'Shifting the geography of reason in an age of disciplinary decadence', *Transmodernity, 1*(2), 6–9.

Gordon, L. R. (2015) *Disciplinary decadence: Living thought in trying times.* London: Routledge.

Grosfoguel, R. (2007) 'The epistemic decolonial turn: Beyond political-economy paradigms', *Cultural Studies, 21*(2–3), 211–223.

Habib, A. (2019) *Rebels and rage: Reflecting on #FeesMustFall.* Johannesburg and Cape Town: Jonathan Ball.

Hanson, J. (2009) 'Displaced but not replaced: The impact of e-learning on academic identities in higher education', *Teaching in Higher Education, 14*(5), 553–564.

Heleta, S. (2016) 'Decolonisation of higher education: Dismantling epistemic violence and Eurocentrism in South Africa', *Transformation in Higher Education, 1*(1), 1–8.

Heleta, S. (2018) 'Decolonizing knowledge in South Africa: Dismantling the 'pedagogy of big lies", *Ufahamu: A Journal of African Studies, 40*(2), 47–65.

Henkel, M. (2000) *Academic identities and policy change in higher education.* London: Jessica Kingsley Publishers.

Hlatshwayo, M. N. (2015) *Social capital and first-generation South African students at Rhodes University* (Master's thesis, Rhodes University, Makhanda, South Africa). Retrieved from http://hdl.handle.net/10962/1466

Hlatshwayo, M. N. (2019a) *'I want them to be confident, to build an argument': An exploration of the structure of knowledge and knowers in Political Studies* (Doctoral thesis, Rhodes University, Makhanda, South Africa). Retrieved from http://hdl.handle.net/10962/92392

Hlatshwayo, M. N. (2019b) 'The organic crisis and epistemic disobedience in South African higher education curricula: Making Political Science relevant', *Alternation, 27*(1), 20.

Hlatshwayo, M. N. and Fomunyam, K. G. (2019) 'Theorising the# MustFall student movements in contemporary South African Higher Education: A social justice perspective', *Journal of Student Affairs in Africa, 7*(1), 61–80.

Hlatshwayo, M. N. and Shawa, L. B. (2020) 'Towards a critical re-conceptualization of the purpose of higher education: The role of Ubuntu-Currere in re-imagining teaching and learning in South African higher education', *Higher Education Research and Development, 39*(1), 26–38.

Hlatshwayo, M. N., Shawa, L. B. and Nxumalo, S. A. (2020) 'Ubuntu currere in the academy: A case study from the South African experience', *Third World Thematics: A TWQ Journal, 5*(1–2), 120–136.

Hlengwa, A. (2019) 'How are institutions developing the next generation of university teachers?', *Critical Studies in Teaching and Learning, 7*(1), 1–18.

Jagarnath, V. (2015) 'Working while black at Rhodes', *Daily Maverick*, 14 April 2015. Retrieved from www.dailymaverick.co.za/opinionista/2015-04-14-working-while-black-at-rhodes/

Jansen, J. (2017) *As by fire: The end of the South African university.* Cape Town: Tafelberg Publishers.

Kamanzi, B. (2016) 'Decolonising the curriculum: The silent war for tomorrow', *Daily Maverick*, 28 April 2016. Retrieved from www.dailymaverick.co.za/opinionista/2016-04-28-decolonising-the-curriculum-the-silent-war-for-tomorrow/

Kamwendo, G. H. (2016) 'Unpacking Africanisation of higher education curricula: Towards a framework'. In V. Msila and T. Gumbo (Eds.), *Africanising the curriculum: Indigenous perspectives and theories* (pp. 17–31). Stellenbosch: African SUNMedia.

Keet, A. (2014) 'Epistemic "othering" and the decolonisation of knowledge', *Africa Insight, 44*(1), 23–37.

Khoza-Shangase, K. (2019) 'Intellectual and emotional toxicity: Where a cure does not appear to be imminent'. In G. Khunou, E. Phaswana, K. Khoza-Shangase and H. Canham (Eds.), *Black academic voices. The South African experience* (pp. 42–64). Cape Town: HSRC Press.

Khunou, G., Phaswana, E. D., Khoza-Shangase, K. and Canham, H. (Eds.). (2019) *Black academic voices: The South African experience*. Cape Town: HSRC Press.

Kumalo, S. H. (2018) 'Explicating abjection – Historically white universities creating natives of nowhere?', *Critical Studies in Teaching and Learning*, 6(1), 1–17.

Kumalo, S. H. (2020) 'Resurrecting the Black Archive through the decolonisation of philosophy in South Africa', *Third World Thematics: A TWQ Journal*, 5(1–2), 19–36.

Le Grange, L. (2019) '*Currere*'s active force and the concept of *Ubuntu*'. In C, Hébert, N. Ng-A-Fook, A. Ibrahim and B. Smith (Eds.), *Internationalizing curriculum studies. Histories, environments, and critiques* (pp. 207–226). The Netherlands: Springer.

Madlingozi, T. (2016) 'On settler colonialism and post-conquest "constitutionness": The decolonising constitutional vision of African nationalists of Azania/South Africa'. Draft paper. Retrieved from www.academia.edu/33747352/On_Settler_Colonialism_and_Post-Conquest_Constitutionness_The_Decolonising_Consti tutional_Vision_of_African_Nationalists_of_Azania_South_Africa

Madlingozi, T. (2018) 'Decolonising "decolonisation" with Mphahlele', *New Frame*, 1 November 2018. Retrieved from www.newframe.com/decolonising-decolonisation-mphahlele/

Mahabeer, P., Nzimande, N. and Shoba, M. (2018) 'Academics of colour: Experiences of emerging Black women academics in Curriculum Studies at a university in South Africa', *Agenda*, 32(2), 28–42.

Makgoba, M. W. (1997) *Mokoko: The Makgoba affair: A reflection on transformation*. Florida Hills, SA: Vivlia.

Maldonado-Torres, N. (2007) 'On the coloniality of being: Contributions to the development of a concept', *Cultural Studies*, 21(2–3), 240–270.

Maldonado-Torres, N. (2016) *Outline of ten theses on coloniality and decoloniality*. Paris: Fondation Frantz Fanon.

Maton, K. (2014) *Knowledge and knowers: Towards a realist sociology of education*. London: Routledge.

Matthews, S. (2018) 'Confronting the colonial library: Teaching Political Studies amidst calls for a decolonised curriculum', *Politikon*, 45(1), 48–65.

Mbembe, A. (2015) 'Decolonizing knowledge and the question of the archive'. Public Lecture given at the Wits Institute for Social and Economic Research (WISER), University of the Witwatersrand, Johannesburg, South Africa. Retrieved from https://wiser.wits.ac.za/system/files/Achille%20Mbembe%20-%20Decolonizing%20Knowledge%20and%20the%20Question%20of%20the%20Archive.pdf

Mbembe, A. (2016) 'Decolonizing the university: New directions', *Arts and Humanities in Higher Education*, 15(1), 29–45.

McKenna, S. and Boughey, C. (2014) 'Argumentative and trustworthy scholars: The construction of academic staff at research-intensive universities', *Teaching in Higher Education*, 19(7), 825–834.

McKenna, S. and Quinn, L. (2012) 'Lost in translation: Transformation in the first round of institutional audits', *South African Journal of Higher Education, 26*(5), 1033–1044.

Mignolo, W. (2011) *The darker side of western modernity: Global futures, decolonial options.* Durham, NC: Duke University Press.

Msila, V. and Gumbo, M. T. (2016) *Africanising the curriculum: Indigenous perspectives and theories.* Stellenbosch: African SUNMedia.

Naicker, C. (2016) 'From Marikana to #feesmustfall: The praxis of popular politics in South Africa', *Urbanisation, 1*(1), 53–61.

Ndlovu-Gatsheni, S. (2013a) 'Decolonising the university in Africa', *The Thinker, 51*, 46–51.

Ndlovu-Gatsheni, S. (2013b) *Empire, global coloniality and African subjectivity.* New York: Berghahn Books.

Ndlovu-Gatsheni, S. (2018a) 'The dynamics of epistemological decolonisation in the 21st century: Towards epistemic freedom', *Strategic Review for Southern Africa, 40*(1), 16–45.

Ndlovu-Gatsheni, S. (2018b) *Epistemic freedom in Africa: Deprovincialization and decolonization.* London: Routledge.

Ngcobozi, L. (2015) '#RhodesSoWhite: An insight', *The Con*, 27 March 2015. Retrieved from www.theconmag.co.za/2015/03/27/rhodessowhite-an-insight/

Nongxa, L. (2020) 'Intellectual laziness and academic dishonesty: A threat to academic freedom?', *South African Journal of Science, 116*(SPE), 1–5.

Nzimande, N. (2017) 'Experiences of challenging heteronormativity in pre-service teacher training at the University of KwaZulu-Natal: A reflective critical incident approach', *South African Journal of Higher Education, 31*(4), 234–248.

Open Stellenbosch Collective. (2015) 'Open Stellenbosch – tackling language and exclusion at Stellenbosch University', *Daily Maverick*, 28 April 2015. Retrieved from www.dailymaverick.co.za/article/2015-04-28-op-ed-open-stellenbosch-tackling-language-and-exclusion-at-stellenbosch-university/

Pett, S. (2015) 'It's time to take the curriculum back from dead white men', *The Conversation*, 8 May 2015. Retrieved from https://theconversation.com/its-time-to-take-the-curriculum-back-from-dead-white-men-40268

Pinar, W. F. (1975) 'The method of "Currere"', *Counterpoints, 2*, 19–27.

Quijano, A. (2007) 'Coloniality and modernity/rationality', *Cultural Studies, 21*(2–3), 168–178.

Ramose, M. (2015) 'Ecology through ubuntu'. In R. Meinhold (Ed.), *Environmental values emerging from cultures and religions of the ASEAN region* (pp. 69–76). Bangkok: Konrad-Adenauer-Stiftung.

Rodney, W. (1973) *How Europe underdeveloped Africa.* London: Bogle-L'Ouverture Publications and Dar-Es-Salaam: Tanzanian Publishing House.

Said, E. (1978) *Orientalism.* New York: Pantheon.

Samuel, M. A. (2017) 'Review of *Africanising the curriculum: Indigenous perspectives and theories*', *Educational Research for Social Change, 6*(1), 87–92.

Spivak, G. C. (2012) *Outside in the teaching machine.* New York: Routledge.

Sultana, F. (2018) 'The false equivalence of academic freedom and free speech', *ACME: An International Journal for Critical Geographies, 17*(2), 228–257.

Tamale, S. (2020) *Decolonization and afrofeminism*. Ottawa: Daraja Press.

Teferra, D. (2020) 'From 'dumb' decolonisation to 'smart' internationalisation', *University World News*, 27 February 2020. Retrieved from https://www.univer sityworldnews.com/post.php?story=20200224054558329

Trowler, P. (2020) *Accomplishing change in teaching and learning regimes: Higher education and the practice sensibility*. Oxford: Oxford University Press.

Vincent, L. (2018) 'Tell us a new story: A proposal for the transformative potential of Collective Memory Projects'. In P. A. Tabensky and S. Matthews (Eds.), *Being at home: Race, institutional culture and transformation at South African higher education institutions* (pp. 21–44). Pietermaritzburg: UKZN Press.

Vincent, L. D. and Hlatshwayo, M. N. (2018) 'Ties that bind: The ambiguous role played by social capital in black working class first-generation South African students' negotiation of university life', *South African Journal of Higher Education*, *32*(3), 118–138.

Wa Thiong'o, N. (1986) *Decolonising the mind: The politics of language in African literature*. Kenya: East African Publishers.

Wolpe, H. (1972) 'Capitalism and cheap labour-power in South Africa: From segregation to apartheid', *Economy and Society*, *1*(4), 425–456.

5 Towards a decolonized school history curriculum in post-apartheid South Africa through enacting Legitimation Code Theory

Paul Maluleka and Neo Lekgotla laga *Ramoupi*

Introduction

In this chapter, we propose an argument for the decolonization of the School History Curriculum (SHC) in post-apartheid South Africa. We do this through the adoption of a decolonial conceptual framework and the Autonomy dimension of Legitimation Code Theory (LCT). First, we discuss how our elected framework symbolizes an epistemic break from colonial epistemology. This is followed by a discussion of the Autonomy dimension. Through our framework and our enactment of Autonomy, we discuss how the SHC was colonized under colonial-apartheid rule. Further, we discuss how after the end of formal colonial-apartheid rule, coloniality through the SHC has continued to undermine indigenous ways of knowing and being. This is despite post-1994 educational reforms moving towards *Ukuhlambulula* of the SHC from its colonial-apartheid past with the hope of re-establishing *seriti sa MaAfrika* (Mphahlele, 2013). [1] Lastly, we propose ways in which the SHC can be decolonized using our framework and the dimension of Autonomy from LCT.

An epistemic break: a critical decolonial conceptual framework

In this section, we seek to set out several key themes from decoloniality theories from which we draw. These include the distinction between coloniality and colonialism, the relationship between coloniality/modernity, the intersectional inequalities that form the colonial matrix of power, the basis for Western universalism, and arguments for pluriversalism and transmodernism that includes but exceeds the Euro-western episteme. Further, we explicate the signal importance of language and culture, and the call for delinking from current geopolitical ways of knowing and thinking.

DOI: 10.4324/9781003106968-5

Colonialism and coloniality

Colonialism was rationalized as a 'civilizing' mission meant to bring about 'development' when in fact it brought about subjection, genocides and epistemicides. This colonialism is 'a disruptive, de-humanizing, and "thingfying" system' (Césaire, 2000, p. 32). However, it is different from coloniality. Coloniality is the *darker side* of modernity that informs and shapes a way of thinking and being that is often hidden and should be unmasked and dismantled (Mignolo, 2011). Maldonado-Torres asserts that:

> Colonialism denotes a political and economic relation in which the sovereignty of a nation or a people rests on the power of another nation, which makes such a nation an empire. Coloniality, instead, refers to a long-standing pattern of power that emerged [because of] colonialism, but that defines culture, labour, intersubjectivity relations, and knowledge production well beyond the strict limits of colonial administrations. Thus, coloniality survives colonialism.
>
> (Maldonado-Torres, 2007, p. 243)

This makes coloniality a period and a lived reality that survives colonialism. Coloniality is reproduced through various institutions, as well as the SHC.

Coloniality/modernity

Coloniality is inseparable from modernity. The coloniality/modernity project is traceable to and characterized by gruesome genocides/epistemicides of indigenous people, especially in the global South. This was achieved through the naturalization of war and normalization of dominations, oppressions, suffering, and the ability of coloniality to refashion itself by hiding what it truly is – an evil, globalized system. Therefore,

> Modernity provides a rhetoric or narrative of progress, but this cannot be replicated in all parts of the world because modernity is built on the foundations of colonialism, or, more accurately, a colonial matrix of power.
>
> (Christie and McKinney, 2017, p. 5)

Intersectional inequalities in the colonial matrix of power

The colonial matrix of power speaks to a set of technologies of subjectivation that consist of four types, which are entangled and work intersectionally. These include control of the economy; control of authority; control of gender and sexuality; control of knowledge and subjectivity (Maluleka, 2021).

As a concept, the colonial matrix of power enables us to understand and explain why the inequalities associated with coloniality/modernity extend beyond the dismantling of colonial administrations and have been so hard to shift. It also enables us to come up with ways regarding how we can dismantle the pervasiveness of coloniality/modernity.

Pluriversalism, transmodernism and the Euro-western episteme

Decolonialists insist that the situatedness of knowledge be recognized. This is a challenge against the claim of universalism by the Euro-western episteme. Therefore, a decolonial epistemic perspective is a 'pluriversal epistemology; an epistemology that delinks from the tyranny of abstract universals' (Mignolo, 2007, p. 159). This is because it seeks to dismantle epistemic racism/sexism by recognizing all parts of the globe as sources of knowledge and theory.

A decolonial epistemic perspective is also for transmodernity because it recognizes epistemic diversity (Grosfoguel, 2013). This is based on 'the need for a shared and common universal project against capitalism, patriarchy, imperialism and coloniality' (Grosfoguel, 2013, p. 88); and the need to acknowledge that all knowledge is situated.

However, this does not mean that the Euro-western episteme should be simply discarded. Thus, decoloniality is concerned with delinking from Euro-western scholarship, rather than reforming it. It is also concerned with intersectionality and ecologies of knowledge as its epistemological approach (see Chapter 2 of this volume).

Language and culture

Culture and language are crucial aspects of the colonial matrix of power. This relates to linguistic and cultural imperialism. Linguistic and cultural imperialism is the idea that certain languages and cultures are more dominant than others. This usually results in linguicide and culturecide.

There is a need to recentre indigenous African languages to form part of the education systems in Africa (Ramoupi, 2014). Thus, there has been an attempt to decolonize these monolingual myths around language and recentre African indigenous languages in African universities (Chaka *et al.*, 2017).

Delinking

Epistemic disobedience as delinking is one of the key concepts of decoloniality. It is used to overcome challenges resulting from the colonial matrix of power towards different ways of knowing and being.

This means challenging Eurocentrism and Westernization of knowledge that hides its locus of enunciation by claiming to be objective, totalizing and universal. It also means *geo- and-body politics* 'necessitate the importance of disobedience in coming up with alternative ways of producing knowledge outside of western normative frameworks' (Maldonado-Torres, 2004). Thus, those who have been dehumanized and depersonalized into *damnes* (cursed people) become central actors in theorizing their existence (Fanon, 1967).

So, to engage in epistemic disobedience is to delink from dominant Euro-western thought, rationality and ideology. It is about the disruption of universalism through changing the 'terms of the conversation' (Mignolo, 2011, p. 24). Decoloniality is the heart of delinking, because:

> Decolonization itself, the whole discourse around it, is a gift itself, an invitation to engage in dialogue. For decolonization, concepts need to be conceived as invitations to dialogue and not as impositions. They are expressions of the availability of the subject to engage in dialogue and the desire for exchange. Decolonization in this respect aspires to break with monologic modernity.
>
> (Maldonado-Torres, 2007, p. 261)

This can be achieved by recognizing that Euro-western epistemology is situated and provincial too. Thus, historiographies contained in the current SHC in South Africa should be viewed as situated, because the historians that have constructed them and the approaches they have used are situated in certain socio-historical realities that are underpinned by Eurocentrism.

It is worth noting that in our articulation of decoloniality we have failed to show how decoloniality can be productively inserted in curriculum knowledge-building. This is because debates about decolonization often fail to sufficiently articulate their position on this. And this can also be said about some discourses in the sociology of education and knowledge.

Therefore, in the next section, we discuss LCT's Autonomy to highlight how it can be used to reposition the decolonial agenda underpinned by a sociological approach to knowledge that is vested in investigating the relations within knowledge and their intrinsic structures towards addressing the knowledge question posed by the decolonial scholarship.

Legitimation Code Theory: Autonomy

LCT is a conceptual toolkit and analytical methodology made up of several 'dimensions' of sets of concepts. LCT builds on, among many others, the scholarships of Basil Bernstein and Pierre Bourdieu (Maton, 2014). LCT views knowledge as both *social* in the sense of being socially created and *real* in the sense of having effects. LCT seeks to counter much of the 'knowledge-blindness' informed by a *false dichotomy* advanced by positivist absolutism and constructive relativism that defines the sociology of education (Maton, 2014), including (we would argue) many of the calls for decolonization.

LCT has three active dimensions, each of which explores a set of different organizing principles that underlie practices, beliefs and dispositions. That is, they all enable 'knowledge practices to be seen, their organizing principles to be conceptualised and their effects to be explored' (Maton, 2014, p. 3). These dimensions are Specialization (Maton, 2014), Semantics (Maton, 2020) and Autonomy (Maton and Howard, 2018, 2021). These dimensions enable researchers and practitioners to get at what lies beneath what is seen and experienced on the surface, for example, in a curriculum. Thus, analysis of these organizing principles can help reveal the 'rules of the game' or 'ways of working, resources, and forms of status' within fields (Maton, 2014, p. 17). Each set of organizing principles is conceptualized through a species of *legitimation code* (*specialization codes, semantic codes, autonomy codes*). These dimensions allow 'fractal application' (Maton, 2014, p. 13), that is, they can be applied in any educational setting at any level.

We have chosen to use concepts from the dimension Autonomy – see Maton and Howard (2018, 2020, 2021) – to examine the motives behind the content selection for the SHC during colonial-apartheid rule, as well as in post-colonial-apartheid South Africa. This is because Autonomy is particularly powerful for showing the basis of integrating different forms of knowledge. Maton (2016, p. 243) summarizes the dimension as follows:

Autonomy explores practices in terms of relatively autonomous social universes whose organising principles are given by *autonomy codes* that comprise relative strengths of *positional autonomy* (PA) and *relational autonomy* (RA). These are mapped on the *autonomy plane* and traced overtime on *autonomy profiles*.

Maton and Howard (2021, pp. 28–29) assert that:

The dimension of Autonomy begins from the simple premise that any set of practices comprises constituents that are related together in particular ways. . . . Put another way, the concepts examine how practices establish different degrees of insulation around their constituents and the ways those constituents are related together.

These different constituents may include actors, ideas and institutions which are related through explicit producers, tacit conventions, and explicitly stated aims. Therefore, these issues are analytically distinguished as:

- *positional autonomy* (PA) between relations between constituents positioned within a context or category and those positioned in other contexts or categories
- *relational autonomy* (RA) between the relations among constituents of a context or category and the relations among constituents of other contexts or categories

(Maton and Howard, 2021, p. 29)

Put very simply, positional autonomy concerns the insulation of content and relational autonomy concerns the insulation of the purpose to which that content it put. Both can be relatively stronger (+) or weaker (−) ; where stronger implies greater insulation and weaker means less insulation. These can be traced on the *autonomy plane*, giving four principal autonomy codes, as shown in Figure 5.1:

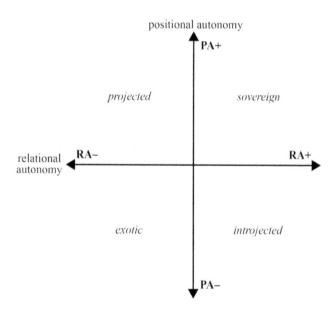

Figure 5.1 The autonomy plane (Maton and Howard, 2018, p. 6).

- *Sovereign codes* (PA+, RA+) exhibit strongly insulated positions and autonomous principles. In other words, valued content emerges from within the context and is used for purposes also coming from within that context.

- *Exotic codes* (PA−, RA−) have weakly insulated positions and heteronomous principles. Hence, content and purposes both come from elsewhere.
- *Introjected codes* (PA−, RA+) have weakly insulated positions but autonomous principles: content that is valued comes from elsewhere but is 'turned to purpose', where that purpose comes from within the context (Maton and Howard, 2020, p. 7).
- *Projected codes* (PA+, RA −) have strongly insulated positions and heteronomous principles: what is valued are constituents from within a context but they are turned to external purposes (Maton and Howard, 2020, p. 7).

In the next two sections, we attempt to highlight how the SHC was colonized under colonial-apartheid rule and continues to be colonized in post-colonial-apartheid South Africa through applying our elected decolonial framework and autonomy codes.

Colonization of the School History Curriculum during colonial-apartheid rule: 1600–1994

Before 1652, different African societies in southern Africa administered different forms of education. For instance, community elders ran initiation and circumcision schools during certain periods of the year and used oral pedagogies in their day-to-day lives to transmit cultural qualities that were often integrated into their life experiences. In 1652, Europeans brought with them *slave education* which was the beginning of the Christianization process of the indigenous people (Maluleka, 2018).

The considered aim of this education was to equip 'slave' children with the basic skills of reading and writing (Education Bureau, 1981, p. 1). However, this education also laid the foundation for socioeconomic and cultural systems that had begun to emerge by the late nineteenth century and are still in place in some forms in contemporary South Africa. These systems are characterized by ecocide, ethnocide, epistemicides, culturecide and linguicide.

The histories taught were informed by Christianity rooted in Euro-western modernity. Thus, Africa and her people were constructed to be in a perpetually primitive condition. The concern of *slave education* was that 'slave' children should be 'well instructed in the fear and knowledge of God and be taught all good arts and morals' (De Chavonnes' Ordinance, 1714, reproduced in Rose and Tunmer, 1975, p. 86). This was oppressive because the 'slave' children were forced to assimilate into new colonial identities. Thus, this eroded social bonding, indigenous beliefs, values, identities, and denied children knowledge of themselves.

This continued with the introduction of *mission education* in the 1800s. This was also a period when many Africans demanded formal education. The British used education as a way of spreading their ways of knowing and being as well as a means of social control (Christie, 1988). The School History (SH) taught was rooted in Euro-western forms of rationality and modernity, which included rote learning that was teacher-centred, authority-driven, content-based, examination-based and elitist (Jansen and Taylor, 2003). This was done to produce 'noble savages' (Hartshorne, 1992). African histories were presented as extensions of Europe in fulfilment of cultural imperialism and as a means of assimilation (Maluleka, 2018).

In 1948 the National Party (NP) came into power and introduced the policy of apartheid. Through Christian National Education (CNE), the NP was able to introduce new ideas of schooling, to oppose and continue some of the characterizations of *slave* and *mission* education. This resulted in the establishment of Afrikaner schools and universities based on ideals of Afrikaner nationalism and CNE.[2] Article 15 of the CNE policy of 1948 explains the basis of apartheid education:

> We believe that the calling and task of White South Africa [about] the native is to Christianise him and help him on culturally, and that. . . [there is] no equality [but] segregation. We believe . . . that the teaching and education of the native must be grounded in the life and worldview of the Whites . . . especially the Boer nation as senior White trustee of the native.
>
> (Msila, 2007, p. 149)

In 1949, D.F. Malan established a Commission of Inquiry into Native Education (referring to indigenous Africans). The main terms of reference for the Commission included 'the formulation of the principles and aims of education for Natives as an independent race' (Rakometsi, 2008, pp. 48–49). This is because the work of the commission was informed by the misinterpretation of the ideology of 'Volkekunde', which is traceable to German anthropologists of the pre-war period such as Muhlmann, and from the Russian Shirokogoroff (Gordon, 1988, p. 536).[3]

The Commission's report was made public in 1951. Its findings were used as a basis for the Bantu Education Act of 1953, which was implemented in 1954. The Act insisted that indigenous Africans be studied and study as distinct groups with unique and separate cultures and geographical locations, as well as 're-tribalize and intensify the de-worlding of Africans by eradicating conditions that produced transcultural "natives" and a creolizing national consciousness' (Madlingozi, 2018, p. 99). Additionally, the Act also insisted on making sure that many of the African youths receive an education. This was partly aimed at easing the 'uncontrollability of these juveniles' which was believed to lead to increased crime rates (Phillip *et al.*, 1993). Moreover, the Act was also aimed at addressing the fear and anxiety of the Commission and government

> that a lack of education in densely populated areas could lead to political mobilization because the government could not regulate the ideas that may be placed in their heads. If these youths could think on their own, they would realize how badly the government treated the blacks in South Africa and they could try to do something about it. The last thing that the government wanted was a challenge to their authority by the urban masses.
>
> (Seroto, 2013, p. 2)

In terms of the SHC, the Final syllabus for History standard 6–8 (Transvaal Education Department, 1967, p. 2) viewed history as based upon the concept of cause and effect, the concept of time and the concept of value of a true record (Seroto, 2013). The syllabus further argued that history teaching is 'to present the past as the living past' and 'to give some idea of the heritage of the past, and the evolution of the present' (Seroto, 2013, p. 2). According to the syllabus, history teachers needed to 'foster an appreciation of certain fundamental values and ideals, such as justice and liberty, through the study of man and nations over a long period of time' (Seroto, 2013, p. 2). The heritage, values and ideals referred to here were all conceptualized from a Eurocentric perspective, thus, Africans and their ways of knowing and being were excluded from the official syllabus.

This is evident from the centering of white men in the content. The history of South Africa was presented as starting with the arrival of Dutchmen in 1652. This shows the extent to which history teaching was misrepresented and used to advance the politics of the day. For instance, the content of the teaching for standard six in the Transvaal was presented in this way:

(i) Van Riebeeck: his significance.
(ii) Simon van der Stel: immigration, expansion, agriculture, Cape-Dutch architecture.
(iii) W. A. Van der Stel: stock-farming, Adam Tas.
(iv) Tulbagh: enlightened despot, beautifying of the Cape Town.
(v) The age of the stock-farmer contact with the Xhosa.

(Seroto, 2013, p. 3)

The teaching of SHC during colonial-apartheid rule prevented indigenous Africans to access 'the truth about whom they really were and where they came from. The ideological underpinning of colonial powers, which suggested that indigenous people were inferior beings, contaminated the education which was provided' (Seroto, 2018, p. 10). Therefore, this can be plotted in the *sovereign code* (PA+, RA+) on the autonomy plane to mean that the curriculum writers of colonial-apartheid SHC sought to not only Christianize and 'civilize'; they also sought to uphold white dominance through their content selection. In other words, they selected knowledge from within their context that they considered being most valuable (PA+) and then made sure that it is taught using the principles that furthered the ends of those who controlled their context (RA+).

Post-colonial-apartheid School History Curriculum

After 1994, stakeholders in SH anticipated a new SHC that was to forge a 'new national identity' (Siebörger, 2000, p. 1). This new SHC was expected to be underpinned by principles of *reconstruction, redress and reconciliation* enshrined in the democratic constitution (Siebörger, 2000). The first democratic Minister of Education, Sibusiso Bhengu, initiated a process of *Ukuhlambulula*, the education system, and putting in place an interim SH syllabus to remove the archaic, racist content that was underpinned by Euro-western forms of rationality and modernity. The democratic government at the time and other stakeholders had to act as *Amatola* – national doctors and diviners – to initiate the *Ukuhlambulula* of the colonial-apartheid SHC to bring about *imvisiswano* – social cohesion – through a process of healing (Tisani, 2018).

This initial process resulted in a new curriculum known as Curriculum 2005 (C2005). An Outcomes Based Education initiative implemented in 1997 as part of the National Curriculum Statement (NCS). It was 'the most radical constructivist curriculum ever attempted anywhere in the world' (Hugo, 2005, p. 22). It was an approach to schooling which unified subjects into learning areas and introduced a completely new approach to education: skills-centred learning and methodological reform. It adopted learner-centred pedagogies, resulting in new methodological approaches and more independent learning processes (Henning, 2016). It was not a subject-bound, content-laden curriculum. Topics were not presented systematically or chronologically like before, they were presented conceptually and thus made the new curriculum open, non-prescriptive and reliant on educators to develop their learning programmes and learning support materials (Chisholm, 2004).

However, this presented difficulties for those with a traditional under-standing of pedagogy and curriculum. Many educators who were reliant on the prescriptions of the colonial-apartheid SHC were now forced to develop their learning programmes and learning support materials, which was something they never did under colonial-apartheid rule because every-thing was provided to them. Many decided to go back to teaching from the colonial-apartheid script because that was what they had access to. This was a result of the lack of preparation of educators moving into peri-urban and rural schools where they did not have strong school and district leadership and were not helped or guided in developing resources. But OBE worked much better in middle-class urban schools where educators had access to Continued Professional Development and support. Therefore, OBE failed largely because the state and the education system did not fully consider how much work was needed to dismantle colonial-apartheid education and rebuild something new in its place, especially given that over 80 per cent of schools were and still are not economically privileged.

Additionally, SH was at risk of losing its identity and was devalued because it was combined with Geography and Civic Education in a learn-ing area known as Humanities and Social Sciences. This was because 'the rejection of the apartheid education [History] curriculum was confused with the abandonment of a curriculum that was based on historically constructed knowledge' (Kallaway, 2012, p. 24). The rationale behind this move was viewed by some as political rather than pedagogical and epistemological. Thus, the Euro-western ways of knowing and being that informed the con-tent remained largely unchallenged and unchanged. Instead of moving the previously marginalized and their ways of knowing and being from the side-lines to the centre, the marginalized under C2005 remained in the mar-gins – side-lined, silenced and de-legitimized.

Kader Asmal succeeded Bhengu in 2000 and initiated the second pro-cess of *Ukuhlambulula* with special attention given to SH due to its impor-tance in contributing to the building of a socially just society. A Ministerial Review Committee, the South African History Project, was appointed and first met in February 2000. An inquiry into School History teaching was also initiated, and the History/Archaeology Panel was established to inves-tigate the teaching of History in schools (Chisholm, 2004). The Ministerial Committee tabled a report that suggested a new SHC and recommended that SH should be integral to the teaching of tolerance.

This process continued and in 2002 a new curriculum known as the Revised National Curriculum Statement (RNCS) was adopted. What set this new curriculum apart from its post-1994 predecessor was that it was consid-ered to have streamlined and strengthened C2005 and was thus committed fully to OBE (Chisholm, 2004). It also sought to foreground a social justice approach that was meant to empower those whose ways of knowing and being were previously marginalized in the SHC. However, it continued to ' "privilege masculinist" interpretations of the past which contributed not only to the general marginalization of women as subjects of History but more importantly it reinforce[d], or ignore[d], oppressive gendered i deas' (Wills, 2016, p. 24).

On the autonomy plane, then, both C2005 and the RNCS can be plotted as shifting, inadvertently, from a *sovereign code* (PA+, RA+) that informed the colonial-apartheid SHC to an *exotic code* (RA –, PA –). The major desire was to weaken relational autonomy (insulation around principles) to allow for the emergence of different voices and different histories to be heard. The intent was to move to a *projected code* (PA+, RA –), whereby content from within a context is used for purposes from beyond that context. However, the delimitation of 'history' as a subject meant that positional autonomy also weakened substantially. What was being taught and to what end were now deeply confused.

A process to review RNCS was thus initiated in late 2008 and early 2009. The third *Ukuhlambulula* process, under the tenure of the successor to Asmal, Naledi Pandor was continued under her successor, Angelina Motshekga who was appointed in 2009. This process resulted in a new curriculum known as the Curriculum and Assessment Policy Statement (CAPS) of 2011, which was part of the National Senior Certificate (NSC) and is currently in use.

However, the prospect of yet another curriculum change was met by suspicion and even rejection. This may be because in-service educators were just over the idea of another curriculum change. It can also be that educators 'often lack the theoretical knowledge and familiarity with principles informing the implementation of curriculum change' (Maharajh *et al.*, 2016, p. 371). Some argued that the on-going curriculum changes were doing more harm than good, while still others argued that the introduction of CAPS symbolized a return to ideas of 'curriculum disciplinarity in the secondary SHC', which represented 'a return to forms of knowledge that experienced teachers would [be] more familiar [with]' (Kallaway, 2012, p. 25). The contention here is that this return affects the decolonial project negatively because the familiarity alluded to here is one that is associated with a colonial-apartheid understanding of curriculum disciplinarity and forms of knowledge.

On the autonomy plane, CAPS can be plotted as moving strongly back into a *sovereign code* (PA+, RA+) from the *exotic code* (RA –, PA –) that informed both C2005 and RNCS – but this time with the intent to foreground previously marginalized histories. However, what is equally evident is that there is a need for SHC to fully delink from the colonial-apartheid past and coloniality/modernity, not only on the political and economic level but also an epistemic level. CAPS has not fully achieved this. Therefore, in seeking to challenge and transcend coloniality/modernity embedded in the current SHC in South Africa; there needs to be an undertaking that would see a deliberate application of decolonial theorizing and thinking to the sovereign code of SH so that different forms of indigenous histories and different ways of indigenous knowing (e.g. oral traditions) can become part of this code rather than being seen as outside of it (introjected or projected). Thus, if the target code is a *sovereign code*, then the decolonial framework we have built here can be used to reset or develop or expand that code, both what constitutes PA (contents) and RA (purposes).

Towards a decolonized School History Curriculum

To transcend coloniality/modernity there must be another process of *Ukuhlambulula* that would entail a commitment from those involved in curriculating and teaching SH through a *policy dialogue* that will seek to centre African scholars whose work was marginalized by colonial-apartheid education; this work will be included and re-historicized within a decolonized SHC. This is necessary because the current Euro-western epistemologies do not have in them the necessary tools to capture, reinterpret, understand, analyze and reconstruct the whole world. The concepts from Autonomy are useful in that they can assist in helping to highlight the power issues at play when content selection is made. This is because they can be enacted to show whose content and whose purposes are valorized or advanced at the expense of others. In so doing, all stakeholders can perhaps come to an agreement that would see greater 'balance' in the content selection process.

Further, there needs to be a commitment to also re-historize histories of women and other marginalized minority groups, such as LGBTQ (lesbian, gay, bisexual, transgender and queer) people, to avoid a 'decolonized' SHC without a *gender-and-other* lens or gaze (Wills, 2016). For instance, Magoqwana speaks about the need to reposition and re-historize *uMakhulu* in the SHC 'as an institution of knowledge that transfers not only "history" through *iintsomi* (folktales), but also as a body of indigenous knowledge that stores, transfers, and disseminates knowledge and values' (Magoqwana, 2018, p. 76).[4] This is a challenge to the monopolization of knowledge production, especially in the academy. It is also a way of reconceptualizing research participants [*oMakhulu*, etc.] as not only information mines, but as co-creators of knowledge. This is because *oMakhulu* have for decades analyzed their social world thus creating knowledge in the process. But, because they may not have used 'academic' theories and concepts, this knowledge exists outside of the academy.

Therefore, there must be an acknowledgement that mere inclusion of work by African scholars, *oMakhulu* and the experiences of other marginalized minority groups in any curriculum does not constitute decolonizing. This means that we must go beyond inclusion; these marginalized intellectual projects must form part of the *nervous system* of a decolonized SHC. By making them part of the nervous system of a decolonized SHC we can begin to recognize that decolonizing curriculum requires us to rethink how the object of study itself is constituted – which is what the autonomy seeks to explore – and thus reconstruct it and bring about fundamental change. This will thus enable us to also confront the theoretical monolithic inadequacies of indigenous knowledge (Mathebula, 2019).

Equally, this will enable us to construct epistemologies, ontologies and methodologies that not only move beyond universal explanations of the world; but embrace trans-modernist and pluriversal explanations of the world and thus are informed and shaped by time and the place, perspective, orientation, and situatedness of their authors. This would result in a SHC that is inclusive, rational and reflective, and make it possible to merge Euro-western and African epistemologies and historiographies to form a decolonized SHC that enables learners and educators to engage with what Hountondji (1997) terms *endogenous knowledge.*[5] Thus, we will move beyond narrow provincialism of knowledge.

Lastly, the question of decolonization also needs to speak to the question of *language* and *pedagogy*. Therefore, African languages need to be institutionalized and academicized if we are to have a decolonized SHC that can contain Africans' thoughts, histories, cultures and experiences, encoded through the languages that they speak (Maseko, 2018). This is because 'if we have to develop knowledge about African societ[ies], it makes sense that we listen to what African languages are saying about their societ[ies]' (Maseko, 2018, p. 36). Moreover, there need to be efforts to reimagine pedagogies that will enable learners to identify and engage with the content they are taught. Therefore, music, oral traditions and other marginalized means of expression need to be considered as tools that can be utilized to decolonize pedagogy. Thus, becoming part of the sovereign code PA (+). For instance, Godsell (2019, p. 22) asserts that poetry can be used 'as a useful tool in decolonizing historical thinking, historical theory, and historical pedagogy', which can result in learners being able to see themselves and feel themselves more in the work done in class.

Conclusion

In *Teaching to transgress: Education as the practice of freedom*, bell hooks argued that:

> The classroom remains the most radical space of possibility in the academy. For years it has been a place where education is being undermined by teachers and students alike who seek to use it as a platform for opportunistic concerns rather than as a place to learn.
>
> (hooks, 1994, p. 12)

hooks further argued that there is a need to collectively 'renew' and 'rejuvenate' how we teach (p. 12). Thus, with this chapter, we have attempted to meaningfully contribute to a collective desire to contribute towards the renewal and rejuvenation of a SHC that is decolonized. This we have done by 'creating bridges' between different knowledges, i.e., LCT from the global North and decolonial scholarship from the global South, to 're-create' the unification of knowledge with the view of realizing the unification of all human beings through the SHC in South Africa (see Hountondji, 1997).

Notes

1 Tisani (2018) conceptualizes *ukuhlambulula* as a process of cleansing, which entails cleansing – inside and outside, touching the seen and unseen, screening the conscious and unconscious. This includes healing of the body and making whole the inner person, because in African thinking "there is an interconnectedness of all things" (Thabede, 2008, p. 238)' (Tisani, 2018, p. 18).

Loosely translated *seriti sa MaAfrika* means the restoration of the dignity of Africans. *Seriti* literally means 'a shadow' – it is also more than an individual's existential quest for appearance. It is a 'life force by which a community of persons are connected to each other' (Muvangua and Cornell, 2012, p. 529).

2 The Afrikaners referred to here are the descendants of the Dutch imperialists, colonists and settlers who arrived in what was known as Cape of Good Hope in 1652, and thus went to establish themselves as a unique people before God with their own civil liturgy, sacred days and leaders.

3 Volkekunde is a discipline of anthropology or an anthropological style or tradition that emerged in South Africa, namely ethnology as practiced by Afrikaans speakers (Seroto, 2013). Dr PJ Coertze (1973, p. 1, quoted in Sharp, 1980), a lecturer at the University of Pretoria, explains that 'Volkekunde studies people as complex beings as they lead a creative existence, following their nature and character, in changing social-organic entities, called etniee (ethnoses), which are involved in a process of active adaptation to a complex environment existing in space and time'.

4 'The term *uMama-Omkhulu* elder mother-shortened to *uMakhulu* [*oMakhulu* in plural] is used in [Nguni languages] as a source of knowledge. Using this term

avoids the inherent epistemological challenges provided by "grandmother" in rein-
serting the notion of "extended family" as the norm' (Magoqwana, 2018, p. 76).
5 Hountondji (1997, p. 17) describes endogenous knowledge as a knowledge
approach that 'create[s] bridges, [and] re-create[s] the unity of knowledge, or in
simpler, deeper terms, the unity of the human being'.

References

Césaire, A. (2000) *Discourse on colonialism* (Trans. by Joan Pinkham). New York:
Monthly Review Press.

Chaka, C., Lephalala, M. and Ngesi, N. (2017) 'English studies: Decolonisation,
deparochialising knowledge and the null curriculum', *Perspectives in Education*,
35(2), 208–229.

Chisholm, L. (2004) 'The history curriculum in the (revised) national curriculum
statement: An introduction'. In S. Jeppie (Ed.), *Towards 'new' histories for South
Africa: On the place of the past in our present* (pp. 177–188). Landsdowne: Juta
Gariep.

Christie, P. (1988) *The right to learn*. Braamfontein, Johannesburg: Ravan Press.

Christie, P. and McKinney, C. (2017) 'Decoloniality and "model C" schools: Ethos,
language, and the protests of 2016', *Education as Change*, *21*(3), 1–21.

Education Bureau (1981) *Education for life*. Cape Town: Department of Internal
Affairs.

Fanon, F. (1967) *Black skin, white masks* (Trans. by C. Markmann), New York:
Grove Press.

Godsell, S. (2019) 'Poetry as method in the History classroom: Decolonising possibilities', *Yesterday&Today*, *21*, 1–28.

Gordon, L. R. (1988) 'The genealogy of Afrikaner anthropology', *American Eth-
nologist*, *15*(3), 535–553.

Grosfoguel, R. (2013) 'The structure of knowledge in westernized universities:
Epistemic racism/sexism and the four genocides/epistemicides of the long 16th
century', *Human Architecture*, *11*(1), 73–90.

Hartshorne, K. (1992) *Crisis, and challenge: Black education 1910–1990*. Cape
Town: Oxford University Press.

Henning, H. (2016) 'Same textbooks – different perspectives: Discussing apart-
heid in two very different South African school settings'. In M. A. Naseem, A.
Arshad-Ayaz, and J. Rodriguez (Eds.), *Representation of minorities in textbooks:
International comparative perspectives* (pp. 59–78). Santiago de Compostella:
Universiade de Santiago de Compostella.

hooks, b. (1994) *Teaching to transgress: Education as the practice of freedom*.
Routledge: New York.

Hountondji, P. J. (1997) *Endogenous knowledge: Research trails*. Dakar: CODESRIA.

Hugo, W. (2005) 'New conservative or new radical: The case of Johan Muller',
Journal of Education, *36*, 19–36.

Jansen, J. and Taylor, N. (2003) 'Educational change in South Africa 1994–2003:
Case studies in large-scale education reform', *Country Studies Education Reform
and Management Publication Series*, *2*(1), 1–47.

Kallaway, P. (2012) 'History in senior secondary school CAPS 2012 and beyond: A comment', *Yesterday&Today, 7*, 23–62.

Madlingozi, T. (2018) *Mayibuye iAfrika? Disjunctive inclusions and black strivings for constitution and belonging in "South Africa"* (Doctoral thesis, Birkbeck College, University of London, London, United Kingdom). Retrieved from http://vufind.lib.bbk.ac.uk/vufind/Record/589681.

Magoqwana, B. (2018) 'Repositioning uMakhulu as an institution of knowledge: Beyond 'biologism' towards uMakhulu as the body of indigenous knowledge'. In J. Bam, L. Ntsebeza and A. Zinn (Eds.), *Whose history counts? Decolonising African pre-colonial historiography* (pp. 75–90). Cape Town: AFRICA Sun MeDIA.

Maharajh, L. R., Nkosi, T. and Mkhize, M. C. (2016) 'Teachers' experiences of the implementation of the Curriculum and Assessment Policy Statement (CAPS) in three primary schools in KwaZulu Natal', *Africa's Public Service Delivery and Performance Review, 4*(3), 371–388.

Maldonado-Torres, N. (2004) 'The topology of being and the geopolitics of knowledge: Modernity, empire and coloniality', *City, 8*(1), 29–56.

Maldonado-Torres, N. (2007) 'On coloniality of being: Contributions to the development of a concept', *Cultural Studies, 3*, 240–270.

Maluleka, P. (2018) *The construction, interpretation, and presentation of King Shaka: A case study of four in-service history educators in four Gauteng schools* (Masters thesis, University of the Witwatersrand, Johannesburg, South Africa). Retrieved from https://hdl.handle.net/10539/26947.

Maluleka, P. (2021) 'Teaching in the time of crisis: A decolonial take of my experiences of online teaching at a rural university in South Africa', *African Perspectives of Research in Teaching & Learning, 5*(1), 78–94.

Maseko, P. (2018) 'Language as source of revitalization and reclamation of indigenous epistemologies: Contesting assumptions and re-imagining women identities in (African) Xhosa society'. In J. Bam, L. Ntsebeza and A. Zinn (Eds.), *Whose history counts? Decolonising African pre-colonial historiography* (pp. 35–57). Cape Town: AFRICA SUN MeDIA.

Mathebula, T. (2019) 'African philosophy (of education) and decolonisation in post-apartheid South African higher education'. In C. H. Manthalu and Y. Waghid (Eds.), *Education for Decoloniality and Decolonisation in Africa* (pp. 1–24). Johannesburg: Palgrave Macmillan.

Maton, K. (2014) *Knowledge and knowers: Towards a realist sociology of education.* London and New York: Routledge.

Maton, K. (2016) 'Legitimation Code Theory: Building knowledge about knowledge-building'. In K. Maton, S. Hood, and S. Shay (Eds.), *Knowledge-building: Educational studies in Legitimation Code Theory* (pp. 1–24). Abingdon, Oxfordshire: Routledge.

Maton, K. (2020) 'Semantic waves: Context, complexity and academic discourse'. In J. R. Martin, K. Maton and Y. J. Doran (Eds.), *Accessing academic discourse: Systemic functional linguistics and Legitimation Code Theory* (pp. 59–85). London: Routledge.

Maton, K. and Howard, S. K. (2018) 'Taking autonomy tours: A key to integrative knowledge-building', *LCT Centre Occasional Paper, 1*, 1–35.

Maton, K. and Howard, S. K. (2020) 'Autonomy: The next phase of dialogue between systemic functional linguistics and Legitimation Code Theory', *Journal of World Languages*, 6(1–2), 91–112.

Maton, K. and Howard, S. K. (2021) 'Targeting science: Successfully integrating mathematics into science teaching'. In K. Maton, J. R. Martin and Y. J. Doran (Eds.), *Teaching science: Knowledge, language, pedagogy* (pp. 23–48). London: Routledge.

Mignolo, W. D. (2007) 'Delinking: The rhetoric of modernity, the logic of coloniality and the grammar of de-coloniality', *Cultural Studies*, 21/2(3), 449–513.

Mignolo, W. D. (2011) 'Geopolitics of sensing and knowing: On (de)coloniality, border thinking and epistemic disobedience', *Postcolonial Studies*, 14(1), 273–283.

Mphahlele, E. (2013) *Afrika my music: An autobiography, 1957–1983*. Cape Town: Kwela Books.

Msila, V. (2007) 'From apartheid education to the Revised National Curriculum Statement: Pedagogy for identity formation and nation building in South Africa', *Nordic Journal of African Studies*, 16(2), 146–160.

Muvangua, N. and Cornell, D. (Eds.). (2012) *uBuntu and the law: African ideals and postapartheid jurisprudence*. New York: Fordham University Press.

Phillip, B., Delius, P. and Posel, D. (1993) *Apartheid's genesis: 1935–1962*. Johannesburg: Witwatersrand University Press.

Rakometsi, M. (2008) *The transformation of black education in South Africa, 1950–1994: A historical perspective* (Doctoral thesis, University of the Free State, Bloemfontein, South Africa). Retrieved from http://hdl.handle.net/11660/1449.

Ramoupi, N. L. L. (2014) 'African languages policy in education of South Africa: 20 years of freedom or subjugation?', *Journal of Higher Education in Africa*, 12(2), 53–93.

Rose, B. and Tunmer, R. (Eds.) (1975) *Documents in South African education*. Johannesburg: Danker.

Seroto, J. (2013) 'A revisionist view of the contribution of Dr Eiselen to South African education: New perspectives', *Yesterday&Today*, 9, 91–108.

Seroto, J. (2018) 'Dynamics of decoloniality in South Africa: A critique of the history of Swiss mission education for indigenous people', *Studia Historiae Ecclesiasticae*, 44(3), 1–14.

Sharp, J. (1980) 'Two separate developments: Anthropology in South Africa', *RAIN*, 36, 4–6. https://doi.org/10.2307/3032180

Siebörger, R. (2000) 'History and the emerging nation: The South African experience', *International Journal of Historical Learning, Teaching and Research*, 1(1), 39–48.

Tisani, N. C. (2018) 'Of definitions and naming: "I am the earth itself. God made me a chief on the very first day of creation"'. In J. Bam, L. Ntsebeza, and A. Zinn (Eds.), *Whose history counts? Decolonising African pre-colonial historiography* (pp. 15–34). Cape Town: AFRICAN SUN MeDIA.

Transvaal Education Department (1967) *Final syllabus for history*, standards 6–8.

Wills, L. (2016) 'The South African high school history curriculum and the politics of gendering decolonisation and decolonising gender', *Yesterday&Today*, 16, 22–39.

6 Decolonization and science education

What is at stake?

Hanelie Adendorff and Margaret A.L. Blackie

Introduction

When writing and talking about decolonization and decoloniality we need to 'begin carefully' and 'walk tenderly along this path of relationships' (Nicol *et al.*, 2020, p. 191), mindful of risks such as misrepresentation and appropriation, yet ready to engage in critical conversations. We have previously shown how different legitimation rules can lead to a 'code clash' in this conversation in science (Adendorff and Blackie, 2020). Decolonial conversations typically foreground the subject and the context (Luckett, Chapter 3, this volume), while science tends to foreground objects, as illustrated in Chapter 7 of this volume. Despite these difficulties, we believe that this conversation offers science the opportunity to bring itself closer to the context of the society in which it operates, and to use its tools and products in the fight for cognitive justice with 'an equality of knowers form[ing] the basis of dialogue between knowledges' (Leibowitz, 2017).

Furthermore, finding solutions to wicked problems, such as poverty, world hunger and global pandemics, will require a concerted and collaborative effort involving science and various other environments, amongst which are indigenous knowledge systems and the humanities. A conversation between science and decolonization scholars is thus neither a luxury nor a threat; rather it is a necessity and an opportunity. However, like the 'two cultures' debate in the 1960s and the 'science wars' that followed that in the 1990s (Burnett, 1999; Gould, 2000; James, 2016; Maton, 2014a), the decolonial conversation in science is often marked by an us–them dichotomy (Gould, 2000). In this chapter, we like Aikenhead and Ogawa (2007, p. 540), hope to 'offer insights of value to science educators so they can build bridges between their own Eurocentric knowledge system and other ways of knowing'.

To do this, we will start by showing various tensions in the literature on decolonizing science. We will follow this by looking at how science and

DOI: 10.4324/9781003106968-6

indigenous knowledge systems (IKS) are portrayed using the concept of *constellations* from LCT (Maton, 2014a; Maton and Doran, 2021), before returning to the need for a conversation. Finally, we will enact the LCT dimension of Specialization to look at specific examples, in order to help us suggest a way forward.

The concepts of decolonization and coloniality in the context of science

Many of the prominent voices in the decolonization debate, such as Aimé Césaire, Ngũgĩ wa Thiong'o, Frantz Fanon, Achille Mbembe and Paulo Freire had roots in the humanities and social sciences or drew from these fields to formulate and communicate their ideas. With this work growing in prominence and extending to other contexts, the terms 'decolonizing', 'colonialism' and 'coloniality' started taking on a variety of complex, and sometimes even contested, meanings (Ideland, 2018; Nicol *et al.*, 2020). It is thus necessary to briefly define the terms we will be using. Colonialism is generally taken to refer to a specific period in time, while coloniality has been described in terms of the longer-lasting attitudinal and ideological impact of colonization (Castro-Gómez, 2002 quoted in Ideland, 2018, p. 786). Colonization, in its most basic form, starts with the physical invasion of a land, with the invasion almost invariably also resulting in the domination and subjugation of the indigenous peoples of that land through 'cultural, social, and economic assimilation. The concept of colonization therefore includes a broad spectrum of contexts in which one culture forcibly imposes itself upon another' (Hassel *et al.*, 2019, p. 4). Coloniality is the more pervasive product of this process, 'expressed in a language of salvation, help, or development' (Ideland, 2018, p. 786).

Decolonization in higher education thus becomes a means of bringing about attitudinal change by breaking with colonial influences and attitudes reflected in our curricula (Cleophas, 2020). To this end, the decolonization conversation in science needs to (1) recognize the way in which scientific knowledge has been shaped by ideology, context and politics and (2) address the 'mutual hostility' arising from this (Cleophas, 2020, p. 2). Various ways to approach this have been suggested. These include, but are not limited to, (1) research with indigenous communities as means of opening up possibilities for translation between Western science and concepts within indigenous knowledge systems (IKS) (Eglash *et al.*, 2020), (2) a greater focus on access, identity and the history of science, i.e., the role science played in colonization practices (Crease *et al.*, 2019), as well as (3) bringing context or place-ness, an awareness of where and how science impacts society, into the often acontextual or placeless science curriculum (Marker,

2019). It is against this background that the decolonization conversation in science needs to be seen. Advancing this conversation, however, requires a way to make sense of the, often heated, exchange between scientists, rooted in their way of seeing and interacting with the world, and decolonization scholars, grounded in very different ways of building knowledge. To this end, we will start by looking at how the way in which science and science education is portrayed and positioned, and is positioning itself, in decolonization literature might be adding to the difficulty.

Science and indigenous knowledge systems in the context of decoloniality

Literature about decoloniality in science tends to pitch science against IKS. For example, science is regularly portrayed as a gatekeeper (Boiselle, 2016) and a 'powerful, colonial weapon' used, among other purposes, to silence Indigenous voices (Ideland, 2018, p. 786) by restricting what is taught or seen as legitimate knowledge (Green, 2012). Prominent themes in the literature include issues of power, i.e., the way science has been, and continues to be, used to exploit others for financial or political gain (Schiebinger, 2009; McClintock, 2013; Boisselle, 2016; Ideland, 2018), issues with epistemological access, identity and cognitive justice, i.e., who can access science and on what grounds (Boisselle, 2016; Ideland, 2018; Cleophas, 2020) as well as issues with the history of science, for example excluding non-Western contributions and failing to acknowledge science's role in colonization (Gould, 2000; Henriques, 2012; Ideland, 2018; Powers, 2020). These works describe science with words such as 'reductionist, secular, and objective/ substantivist' (Boisselle, 2016, p. 5). By contrast, IKS is presented as the relational, non-reductive, more situated 'antithesis of colonial' practices (ibid., p. 6). The risk with such 'othering' and 'counter-othering' strategies (Rip, 2019) is that it could create a situation in which one cannot value one, i.e., indigenous knowledge, without devaluing the other, i.e., Western/ formal science. It does not allow for a both-and approach (Maton, 2016, p. 47) in which science and indigenous knowledges could find a way to collaborate (Green, 2012; Boisselle, 2016; Rip, 2019). Rip (2019) and Green (2012) have independently argued that such a collaboration could help science gain an improved understanding of the context in which its products find application, while it might assist IKS in becoming more available or 'cosmopolitan' (Rip, 2019). However, while some commend the new agreements about 'the nature of reality' (Green (2012, p. 2) this could lead to, others hold that removing indigenous knowledges from their contexts would render them meaningless (Bishop, 1990). So, not only are science and other ways of knowing, such as IKS, seen as opposing forces, but there doesn't seem to be agreement on how they should relate. Elements of the science–IKS portrayal is ominously reminiscent of the so-called science wars of the 1990s and the preceding two-cultures debate, both of which display a similar divide, defined by 'mutual incomprehension', between science and the humanities (Burnett, 1999).

The 'two cultures' debate and the science wars

Gould (2000) describes the science wars as an academic battle between 'realists' and 'relativists', with the realist position being most prominent among scientists and relativist position mostly seen among staff 'housed in faculties of the humanities and social sciences' (p. 253). The realist position focussed on the objectivity of science while the relativist position focused on 'the culturally embedded status of all claims' which would make science 'just one system of belief among many alternatives' (p. 253). Babich (2017) contends that what was at issue was legitimacy: 'who should be permitted to speak and who should be silenced' (Babich, 2017, p. 167). The so-called 'two cultures' debate between scientists and scholars from the humanities, which preceded the science wars, began in the late 1950s with the work of C.P. Snow and F.R. Leavis (James, 2016). This exchange presented the world as two 'noncommunicating cultures' – science and the humanities – which interacted by little more than 'hostile glares' (Burnett, 1999). Like the science wars, this debate stemmed from a power struggle between two camps using different epistemic logics to legitimize their practices (Maton, 2014a). The scientists in the debate were viewed as sharing 'a sense of loyalty to an abstraction called "knowledge"' (Mackerness, 1960, quoted by Maton, 2014a, p. 72) as well as a 'commitment to "truth" and allegiance to their discipline, which specialized their identity and claims to insight, regardless of their social backgrounds or personal attributes' (ibid., p. 72). The humanist culture in the debate was constructed as placing far less emphasis on knowledge. The specialized skills and knowledge required for legitimacy in science, was relatively unimportant in defining legitimacy in the humanities; what mattered here was 'possessing the right kind of dispositions or character' (ibid., p. 73); that is, being the right kind of 'knower'. The 'two cultures' debate can thus be depicted as a 'code clash' (Maton, 2014a) and struggle for supremacy between two fields with different underpinning legitimizing logics.

The more recent decolonial conversation, as it pertains to science, displays a similar dichotomy and struggle for supremacy. Interestingly, the early developers of modern science did not observe the dichotomy we see in discussions of science today (Gould, 2000). Instead, they saw the understanding they were seeking as arising from both the mind of the scientists and the experiment, thus combining the scrutiny of one's own 'internal biases, both mental and social' and the observation of nature. It follows then that, from this vantage point, science does not build knowledge 'outside the social order and despite its impediments', but within the space of human relations (Gould, 2000, p. 255). Gould (2000) thus holds that the science– humanities divide might be viewed as little more than a false dichotomy resulting from naïveté about the history of science.

In his blog entitled *Revisiting the Science Wars*, Henriques (2012, para 6 and 7) similarly cautions against seeing science as a set of social con- structions only, suggesting instead that we look at science as a justification system 'comprised of both analytic and normative components'. Literature, however, abounds with dichotomizing descriptions of science as either objective and acontextual or science as merely a set of social constructions. This is most notably manifested in science being portrayed as 'against' something: against the ancient philosophies of perfection, against religion, against humanities in the so-called 'science wars' (Gould, 2000) and most recently against indigenous knowledges, displayed as a battle between the West (science) and the Rest (indigenous knowledges) (Aikenhead and Ogawa, 2007).

The LCT dimension of Specialization (Maton, 2014a) offers a heuris- tic that can help us drill beneath the surface of this objective realism and social constructionism divide in these discourses. Specialization allows a means of unravelling the relations between knowledge and knowers in dif- ferent knowledge-building practices. In this case, it can help to shed light on the logics underpinning the apparent dichotomy. We could, for example, use Specialization to argue that the social constructionist position valorizes the knower as the basis for legitimacy, thus placing emphasis on the social aspects such as context and knower subjectivity, while the objective realist position valorizes the more objective, explanatory aspects of knowledge. But Specialization also helps us to understand that despite what a field may valorize or emphasize, all fields consist of *both* knowledge *and* knowers. So, whilst legitimacy in science is more closely related to the epistemic ele- ments of the practice, the social elements of this practice cannot be ignored (see Chapter 7).

One way of addressing the polarized set of views is through critical con- versations that would include topics on the history, philosophy and sociol- ogy of science. Such conversations would allow us to address issues such as concept of objectivity and the acontextual nature of science. It could, for example, open spaces to engage with the idea that science 'maximises, but does not achieve, objectivity' through minimising 'the subjectivities of individual scientists and of tradition in that community' (Aikenhead and Ogawa, 2007, p. 546), and allow us to explore the position that scientific

endeavour can be likened to a 'dance of agency' or 'back and forth negotiation' between scientists and nature, in which knowledge is 'constantly
produced and reproduced in interactions' (Green, 2012). Similarly, a better
understanding of the history of science can 'help legitimize the role of science in society' whilst 'enhanc[ing] the professional identity or credibility
of science' (Powers, 2020, p. 581), both of which are critical steps in repositioning science in the cognitive and social justice conversation.

Through this chapter, we hope to show some ways in which 'polarised
thinking' (Vandeyar and Swart, 2019, p. 776), for example, seeing science
as either purely objective or purely socially constructed, or seeing science
as a problem and IKS as a solution, can be 'dismantled' in order to enable a
constructive conversation.

The conversation about decolonization and science

We have already established that the divide between science and humanities seen in the two-cultures debate and the science wars also extends to
the decolonial conversation in science. Green (2012), for example, warns
against (1) defining the knowledges in science and IKS as so different
that there is 'very little chance of discovering the linkages and partial
connections that might begin a new conversation' (p. 6), and (2) thinking that 'either all ways of knowing the world, including the sciences,
are belief, or all are knowledge' (p. 7), the dichotomy at the heart of the
science wars. Even though a 'dichotomous discourse' might at times be
necessary to help us 'act politically' (Rip, 2019, p. 90), finding a shared
ground from which to respond to the ways in which African knowledges,
histories of knowledge and ways of knowing have been and are still
being marginalized (Gould, 2000; Green, 2012; Rip, 2019) would greatly
benefit from a less dichotomized approach. The dichotomous othering/
counter-othering and us/them portrayal of science in literature and in
decolonization conversations thus poses a significant challenge to finding a productive opening or starting point for decolonial conversations in
science (see Green, 2012).

The breakdown in the #ScienceMustFall (#SMF) conversation has been
attributed to multiple deep disagreements in the 'conversational thread',
resulting from a 'historical lack of constructive engagement and dialogue
between scientific thinking and cultural beliefs' (Ally and August, 2018,
p. 355) as well as a code clash originating in the legitimation practices used
by different role players in the conversation (Adendorff and Blackie, 2020).
Just as Green (2012) has argued for a 'translation' between different kinds
of knowledges, we have called for mediation between scientists and those
calling for decolonization (see Adendorff and Blackie, 2020).

Legitimation Code Theory offers a number of analytical tools for investigating the knowledge practices underpinning science and decolonization. In a previous study, we employed Specialization to uncover reasons for the breakdown in the decolonization conversation (i.e., the code clash we have mentioned). We will now drill deeper into nature of the science IKS dichotomy, using the concept of *axiological constellations* to analyze the problem and suggest a way forward.

Building knowledge with constellations

The concept of *constellations* analogizes to the familiar idea of grouping stars into recognizable images to help explain how actors shape what is seen as legitimate in a field (Maton, 2014a; Maton and Doran, 2021). The stars that form part of a constellation are selected from a vast array of possible celestial objects and are not necessarily in close proximity to one another, although they might appear so when viewed from Earth. Ideas, objects, values and beliefs, just like stars, can be grouped together to form constellations that can help us navigate the knowledge in a field or knowledge practice. The way in which this happens is determined by the cosmology of the intellectual field doing the *constellating*. All intellectual fields have *cosmologies* or worldviews, the ways in which they make sense of the world, for example whether there is an 'objective' truth to be discovered or whether all 'truth' is situated and relative. These worldviews act like the vantage points in that they determine what we see and how we group ideas to make sense of them. If we believe that there is an objective truth to be discovered, we are likely to design our experiments from that perspective and fail to account for the role of our own subjectivity in the chosen design. To help us make sense of the cosmologies that underpin knowledge practices, and the constellations that they lead to, we need to start with the concept of Specialization.

Starting from the perspective that all knowledge practices involve both knowledge and knowers, Specialization is concerned with what counts as a legitimate knowledge claim and who is allowed to make such claims, in other words who would be counted as legitimate knowers (Maton, 2014a). It thus sets up two relations: *epistemic relations* (ER) concerned with knowledge, and *social relations* (SR) concerned with knowers. These relations form the basis for deciding what counts as legitimate knowledge and who counts as a legitimate knower. Different knowledge practices emphasize these relations in different ways. In other words, practices may place a greater emphasis on either epistemic relations or social relations or both or neither. Practices that valorize epistemic relations will place a greater value on possession of specialist knowledge, such as scientific knowledge while practices that valorize social relations will place greater value of the attributes of the knower. Since both can vary from weaker to stronger, we can plot these two relations on a plane and analyze practices in terms whether they emphasize one, both or neither as the basis for status and achievement. Stronger epistemic relations (ER+) coupled with weaker social relations (SR –), i.e., where practices emphasize the possession of specialized skills, knowledge and procedures as the basis for success whilst downplaying the attributes of the actor making the claim, yield a *knowledge code*. Conversely, with weaker epistemic relations (ER+) coupled with stronger social relations (SR –), i.e., when what you are studying and how is less important than who you are and what kind of interactions you were shaped by, we have a *knower code*. Where both epistemic and social relations are both relatively weak, we have a *relativist code* and when both are relatively strong, an *élite code*.

Social fields can thus be understood as *knowledge–knower structures* (Maton, 2014a): all knowledge practices include *both* knowledge *and* knowers. What differs is how these are organized and what (and who) is valorized. Scientists are not absent from the knowledge project in science, but their attributes are not generally used as a basis for success. Knowledge practices in knowledge-code fields (like those often found in the sciences) are underpinned by an *epistemological cosmology*, giving rise to *epistemological constellations* where ideas, objects, practices and beliefs are organized around their ability to coherently explain observations.

In knower-code fields, such as the fields underpinning decolonization scholarship (Luckett, Chapter 3, this volume), we often find *axiological cosmologies* where value-laden meanings are grouped together to form *axiological constellations*. In both cases, the meanings that are clustered together are also selected from a vast field of possibilities, tracing boundaries that will exclude some meanings and include others. *Axiological constellations* thus represent connected groups of value-laden meanings that are used to make sense of or navigating a knowledge field.

The concept of constellations also draws on the LCT dimension of Semantics as we have just shown 'to distinguish epistemological and axiological forms of condensation whereby stances are imbued with meanings that are then differentially charged with legitimacy' (Maton, 2014a, p. 150). Semantics focuses on how meanings are made and introduces two concepts to that end: semantic gravity and semantic density. *Semantic gravity* (SG) describes the degree of context-dependence of meanings and it may be stronger (+) or weaker (–) along a continuum of strengths. 'The stronger the semantic gravity (SG+), the more meaning is dependent on its context; the weaker the semantic gravity (SG –), the less dependent meaning is on its context' (Maton, 2014b, p. 2).

Semantic density (SD) refers to the degree to which meaning is packed into the terminology used in a practice and may be stronger (+) or weaker (–) along a continuum of strengths. With stronger semantic density (SD+), more meanings will be condensed into the terminology in that practice; while practices with weaker semantic density (SD –), will have terminology that have fewer meanings condensed into it (Maton, 2014b, 2020). Returning to the concept of constellations, meanings in *epistemological constellations* will be epistemologically condensed (with explanatory meanings), while meanings in *axiological constellations* will be axiologically condensed (strong connections of moral meanings).

We have previously shown that decolonization conversations tend to downplay explanatory power whilst emphasizing moral virtue (Adendorff and Blackie, 2020). In this chapter, we are interested in exploring the way in which this is the result of a specific kind of constellating, the consequence of which is a dichotomous portrayal of science and IKS in literature.

Constellation analysis of the IKS–science binary in decolonization literature

There is a growing body of literature that compares and contrasts Modern Western Science (also called modern science knowledge systems (Tharakan, 2017)) and Eurocentric sciences (Aikenhead and Ogawa, 2007), with IKS (also called by various other names, such as traditional knowledge, indigenous technical knowledge, local knowledge, ecological knowledge and sometimes people's science, with much debate about what would be most appropriate, see for example Tharakan, 2017 and Mazzocchi, 2006) often setting them up as binaries. A constellation analysis of these depictions of science in the decolonization literature can show how the concepts related to 'Modern Western Science' and 'indigenous knowledge systems' are part of two binary constellations (see Table 6.1). In places where such dichotomous constellations are constructed it usually implies that agreeing or associating with one element in one of the constellations means agreeing with all the others as well. For example, seeing the world from a realist perspective implies also holding an anthropocentric view that sees nature as a servant to humankind (Aikenhead and Ogawa, 2007). Looking at Table 6.1, we see another instance of a code-clash, here between the underpinning axiological cosmology (value-laden connections of meanings) manifested in topics such as modern/postmodern, localized/globalized and the epistemological cosmology typically underpinning science (premised on explanatory power). This is especially well represented in the position offered by Cleophas (2020) who 'rejects an over emphasis on knowledge content as a vehicle for understanding', instead aiming to 'challenge deep

Table 6.1 Indigenous knowledge systems vs Modern Western Science constellations in the literature used in this study

Indigenous knowledge systems	Modern Western Science
Postmodern	**Modern**
Monist	Cartesian Dualist
Relativist	Objectivist, Positivist
Social constructivist	Realist
Post-colonial	Colonial
Post-human	Humanist, Anthropocentric
Holistic	Reductionist
Local	**Global**
Socially embedded	Socially distanced
Multicultural, Differentiated	Universalist
Place-based	Place-less
Community focused/local	Globalized
Context aware	Abstracted
Relational	Competitive
Relational	**Anthropocentric**
One with nature	In control of nature
Value circulation	Value extraction
Nature as self-modifying	Nature as static
Environmentally sustainable	Environmentally destructive
Subjective	Authoritarian
Spiritual	Secular
Embodied	Disembodied
Time as circular	Time as linear

assumptions, beliefs and values that hold institutional knowledge and values in place' (p. 2).

The ideas or stances listed in Table 6.1, drawn from the sources used in this chapter, are not disparate but reflect an underlying cosmology (see Maton, 2014a). In order to makes sense of this cosmology, we have organized the stances into more coherent groups, reflecting the key points of opposition: postmodern–modern, local–global, relational–anthropocentric. We will now unpack the sets of stances in Table 6.1 to further elaborate on this cosmology and its implications for the conversation between decolonization discourses and science.

Modern–postmodern

The terms 'modern' and 'modernity' have been closely linked to colonization and colonialism (see for example Boiselle, 2016). Here, the modern–postmodern tension pits science as an oppressive 'colonial', 'reductionist' and 'dualist' commercial exploiter and gatekeeper, with a subjugating role, against all indigenous knowledges as the oppressed, 'holistic', 'relativist' and culturally aware, position which is respectful of multiple ways of knowing and being (Dube, 2019). It captures the objective–subjective divide and draws on the idea of science as a 'hegemonic' and 'powerful' weapon used to silence the indigenous voices, by positioning itself as the only valid way of knowing.

Global–local

The global–local tension sees science as 'globalized', 'socially distant', 'placeless' or contextually unaware or blind and competitive, operating in the decontextualized, theoretical domain while it views IKS as 'community focussed', 'socially embedded', 'place-based' or contextually aware and 'relational' as well as more accessible through operating in the lived-world context.

Anthropocentric–relational

This tension pitches IKS, as in tune with nature, versus science, as in control of nature. It depicts science as an 'authoritarian', 'environmentally destructive' and self-serving enterprise with IKS portrayed as 'environmentally sustainable' and 'subjective' or in harmony with our natural resources and more focussed on the greater good.

Constellating practices

Axiological cosmologies are constellated through four main processes (Doran, 2019): (1) positioning, which includes mentioning the source of a position and showing things from alternative perspectives; (2) oppositioning, which involves putting something up as opposition in order to take it down; (3) likening; and (4) charging positions, either positively or negatively.

Positioning

Positioning can happen through acknowledging a source as well as through presenting alternative perspectives, 'hint[ing] at the tensions that underpin the texts' (Doran, 2019, 30min:43s), i.e., Eglash *et al.* (2020, p. 1346) do this by positioning IKS first from Latour's perspective and then giving the alternative 'Indigenous perspective', indeed pointing to the underlying tension found throughout literature:

> **Latour's claim** is that science creates innovation because it allows hybridity, whereas Indigenous knowledge is static because animism freezes society in accordance with fixed categories in nature. As noted previously (Eglash, 1997), Latour is assuming a Western perspective in which nature is static. **From an Indigenous perspective** nature is full of self-modifying unpredictability.
>
> (emphasis added)

Oppositioning

Oppositioning pits one position against the other usually with the purpose to cast down one. In this excerpt from Boisselle (2016), indigenous knowledges from various sources are set up as diverse, spiritual and relational in opposition to science which is portrayed as reductionist, secular and objectivist:

> First Nations people like the Inuit and Hopi of North America, and the Nepuyo of Trinidad practice a relational science **in comparison with** WMS [Western Modern Science] which is reductionist, secular, and objective/substantivist'.
>
> (Boisselle, 2016, p. 5, emphasis added)

Charging

In Boisselle's 2016 text, this move of oppositioning supports the negative charging of science and the positive charging of IKS, i.e., calling the former flawed:

> the standard account of science is not just Western and modern but also secular in its disposition as it continues to negate the impact/role of Spirit or God in any form in its activities. It is suggested that Western knowledge (as is WMS) might be **flawed** on two counts'.
>
> (Boisselle, 2016, p. 4)

Likening

Likening 'sets up oppositions that appear to group together' (Doran, 2019, 35min:44s). Eglash *et al.* (2020, p. 1346) group together the idea of science as anthropocentric (controlling nature) with concepts of value-extractive environmental destruction (poor models and practices such as mass production agriculture) and nature as static, appearing in the anthropocentric-relational group in Table 6.1:

> It is the Western view that has, in many ways, based its assumptions on **static**, linear frameworks: technical obsessions with **optimization, linear control, routinization**, and so on lead to poor models and practices such as **mass production** agriculture.
>
> (emphasis added)

Seeing the constellations set up in these processes, found throughout STS and decolonization literature, helps us understand some of the difficulty with the conversation and why science might struggle, or might even be reluctant, to engage in it. However, whilst these constellations form a necessary part of critiquing and understanding the sociology of science, they also create a binary that is problematic to bridge. Even so, the process of forming axiological constellations is not the problem here; the problem is failing to recognize these processes as part of the logics of knowledge practices. With recent literature on decolonizing science stemming mostly from the fields of STS, humanities and the social sciences, all underpinned by axiological cosmologies, what is valued – both in terms of legitimacy and how meaning is made or knowledge is created – in these texts differs substantially from what happens in science with its epistemological cosmology. With recent literature on decolonizing science stemming mostly from the fields of STS, humanities and the social sciences, all underpinned by axiological cosmologies, what is valued in these texts – both in terms of legitimacy and the manner in which meaning is made or knowledge is created – differs substantially from what happens in science with its epistemological cosmology. It stands to reason that scientists would read these texts through the filter of their epistemological cosmology, looking for the different constellating principles applying there. Understanding this might help us find a way to advance the conversation in science. Consider the example of the South African government's initial handling of the AIDS crisis in the early to mid-2000s. Although the government at the time was correct in recognizing the importance of attending to the social issues pertaining to the crisis, their denial of what science could offer (Green, 2012; Broadbent, 2017) came at a great cost despite the presumed governmental motivation of a virtuous decolonial agenda (Broadbent, 2017). What we can learn from this is that the solution to problems such as these will require moving beyond dichotomies such as local–global, scientific–traditional, good–bad, a process that will need to start with the role-players (i.e., scientists and decolonization scholars) agreeing to what might be a difficult conversation and having access to tools or analyses, like the one offered in this chapter, that could help to mediate the conversation.

Taking the conversation forward

We have elsewhere proposed that the code clash in the conversation about decolonizing science might be mediated through using facilitators that can shift the codes of their messages to match that of the intended audience (Adendorff and Blackie, 2020). In this chapter, we have showed how the cosmologies or worldviews underpinning the calls for decolonization from within science and the humanities set up an axiologically charged dichotomy between science and indigenous knowledges that is not easy to navigate. In a study that investigates the equally dichotomous climate change conversation, Glenn (2015) suggests that there are two ways in which conversations can be productive in overcoming such clashing or opposing binaries: translating and transforming. In translation strategies the messenger acts as a mediator, translating between the viewpoints of the different parties involved in the conversation. Translating can happen in a number of ways, the first of which involves recognizing the different 'languages' or Specialization codes in the conversation and 'translat[ing] between them' (ibid., p. 209) by shifting the code of the message to match the audience's code. This requires someone to 'translat[e] between languages on behalf of the audience, or in LCT terms, matching the audience's codes' (ibid., p. 209), the audience here being science (and scientists). In the decolonial conversation in science, this would imply translating between the knower-code, axiological cosmology underpinning decolonization calls and knowledge code, epistemological axiology of scientists. Another way to achieve this is to use messengers who share the intended audience's cosmology, who thus do not need to shift codes to translate messages. In this instance, translating might even involve not mentioning the dichotomous topic, i.e., decolonization, but instead requiring the audience to take action for 'other reasons', though ultimately still addressing the issue at hand. In the decolonial conversation in science education, useful frames for this purpose could be understanding how cultural influences might impact science learning or charting a sustainable future for the Earth (Aikenhead, 2017). Both of these approaches, as well as Green's (2012) suggestion of IKS helping science connect with its context, could provide useful motivations for change that do not necessarily require the audience (science) to completely change its cosmology and align with all the beliefs underpinning the IKS constellation. It might, however, open a door for engaging with some of the beliefs underpinning the IKS cosmology, without setting the two up as binary oppositions.

Transformation is interested in changing people's views and actions and is thus typically a slower and more challenging process since it 'requires the audience to learn to speak multiple languages and shift between them, or at least to adopt useful features of the new language' (Glenn, 2015, p. 209). For science, this would imply shifting towards a knower code, to be better able to understand and act on the decolonization calls.

We will now briefly comment on our own experience with utilizing translation during decolonization discussions with various science-based audiences. Drawing on our experience in seven unexpectedly productive conversations, and the principles laid out in this chapter, we will show how the forms of translation offered by Glenn (2015) functioned to advance these conversations in science (for an example of one such a conversation, see Adendorff (2018)).

Shifting the code of the message to match the audience's code

The purpose of this translative action is to reduce resistance by making the topic, in this case the decolonization conversation, feel less alien through matching the code of the message with the audience's legitimation codes. In science this would imply foregrounding and strengthening epistemic relations – specialized knowledges and skills – or using a knowledge code as basis for legitimacy in the conversation. In our case, we did this by focusing on 'making sense of the decolonization conversation' and offering an analytical tool, LCT, to help us do that. With its ability to be used in a technical or empirical way, exhibiting stronger epistemic relations, LCT can help us make the conversation feel less foreign to scientists. Here employed for its explanatory power, LCT thus offers an approach that not only speaks a language closer to that of science, but might prove enticing. Epistemic relations were emphasized and strengthened throughout these sessions when the tools from the LCT dimensions of Autonomy and Specialization were employed and enacted. Although we foregrounded social relations when the topic of decolonization was introduced, for example explaining that the sessions were about opening up a conversation and figuring out how we can start a conversation about decolonizing science education (see, for example, Adendorff, 2018, September, 6), we did not offer it as the basis for legitimate participation in the conversation. With these actions, we located the conversation in science's reason-based epistemology rather than the value-based cosmology of decolonization scholarship.

Messengers who share the audience's cosmology

This approach assumes that there will be different ways of viewing the decolonization conversation in science and thus works to activate these alternative positions through communication. We, as the authors of this chapter and facilitators of these conversations, are both scientists who have gained legitimacy in science through acquiring the prerequisite specialized skills, as evidenced in science PhDs. However, we both have some experience and legitimacy in the social science context too, through immersion in the higher education studies canon and interaction with noted works and scholars. We thus both have access to the epistemological cosmology underpinning science and can make sense of the axiological cosmologies underpinning the social sciences and humanities. Glenn (2015) suggests that this approach of matching the audience's cosmology works best when the messenger uses helpful frames and discourses that are supportive of the goal of the conversation, reframing the decolonization conversation as 'good' and necessary. In our discussions on decolonizing science curricula, we postulated that the alienation that some students experience in science courses could be a useful approach for drawing participants who were reluctant to engage in decolonization conversations into the discussion. Starting the conversation using the epistemology of science, we could show the scientists that we 'spoke their language', opening a space in which we could activate motivations such as finding ways to help students access the field or contributing to sustainable living.

In conclusion, we found that LCT acted both as a theoretical framework or mediatory agent and as a legitimizing tool. Using the explanatory power of LCT as an analytical tool helped to strengthen epistemic relations, thus legitimizing the conversation as something sufficiently close to what counts in science. We believe that this strategy of offering an explanatory framework through which scientists can make sense of the axiologically charged knower code conversation can create a space in which a conversation could grow into dealing with increasingly complex topics. We thus suggest that the conversation can be mediated through a few code shifts and a deep enough understanding of both the knowledge and knower codes involved as well as the resulting constellations to be able to translate the calls for decolonization calls into the science context. Anecdotal feedback from scientists who attended the decolonization discussions in which we applied these analytical tools mentioned that the more epistemically strengthened approach offered by LCT removed the emotive elements from the conversation, and this was one of the reasons for a greater readiness to participate in the conversation. In the words of one of these participants: 'I've sat in a number of these decolonizing fora and discussions and I think as a scientist this is the first time that I feel it has made some sense to me' (Adendorff, 2018, 44min:50s).

Conclusions

In this chapter, we have shown the appeal of the stronger epistemic relations or explanatory power of LCT in the science context. It not only served as a mediatory tool in conversations about decolonizing science, but also as a legitimizing tool, strengthening the epistemic and discursive relations of the message offered by the facilitators. In using the tools offered by Specialization especially, we may avoid the risk of knowledge-blindness (Maton, 2014a) associated with treating decolonization in science in much the same way as decolonization in other fields. Given that the literature relating to decolonizing science is ambiguous and varied, understanding the differences between the meaning making practices in science and those in other fields can help us chart a course for a more successful conversation in science. We have found that the more analytical approach offered by LCT can reduce the emotive elements from the conversation, thus proving an unexpectedly useful tool for mediating the decolonization conversation in science contexts.

Green (2012, p. 1) argues that a conversation is needed 'both in the sciences and the humanities if universities are to be able to respond to the continued marginalisation of African intellectual heritages in the region'. We would add that such a conversation could start with the premise that neither science nor IKS would need to become the other, but that both can learn from the other. This will enable science, the humanities and IKS to retain their unique ontologies and epistemologies, though not uncritically, drawing on the strengths of both. We have shown, through the constellation analysis, that the current dichotomous argumentation is doing little to advance either IKS or science. Solving the real world problems in the global South requires not only the products of science (e.g., vaccines and cell phones), but also the social understanding of the humanities and the contextual awareness of IKS. Thus, these conversations need to be constructed to enable this dichotomy to be challenged and bridged.

We contend that science needs to be repositioned not in opposition to the humanities and IKS, but as a collaborator with other knowledge practices. We have seen the harm done when the products of science are exploited (or devalued) by those with or reaching for political or economic power. We argue, along with Gould (2000), Green (2012) and Powers (2020), that science education needs to pay more attention to the history, philosophy and position of science in society. We cannot wish away or undo the harm done by the naïve or wilful ignorance or worse, of those wielding the powerful weapon of science during the period of colonization. Perhaps then we can wish for a better future, one which the humanities and IKS can help us move towards using the products of science as equally powerful weapons in the fight for cognitive justice (see for example Tamarkin's (2017) work on DNA testing).

References

Adendorff, H. (2018) 'Decolonising the science curriculum: Can Legitimation Code Theory show a way forward?' 6 September. Retrieved from www.sun.ac.za/english/learning-teaching/ctl/t-l-resources/t-l-seminars.

Adendorff, H. and Blackie, M. A. (2020) 'Decolonizing the science curriculum: When good intentions are not enough'. In C. Winberg, S. McKenna and K. Wilmot (Eds.), *Building knowledge in higher education: Enhancing teaching and learning with legitimation code theory* (pp. 237–254). London: Routledge.

Aikenhead, G. S. (2017) 'Enhancing school mathematics culturally: A path of reconciliation', *Canadian Journal of Science, Mathematics and Technology Education, 17*(2), 73–140, DOI: 10.1080/14926156.2017.1308043

Aikenhead, G. S. and Ogawa, M. (2007) 'Indigenous knowledge and science revisited', *Cultural Studies of Science Education, 2*(3), 539–620.

Ally, Y. and August, J. (2018) '#Sciencemustfall and Africanising the curriculum: Findings from an online interaction', *South African Journal of Psychology, 48*(3), 351–359.

Babich, B. (2017) 'Hermeneutics and its discontents in philosophy of science: On Bruno Latour, the "science wars", mockery, and immortal models'. In B. Babich (Ed.), *Hermeneutical philosophies of social science* (pp. XX–XX). The Netherlands: De Gruyter.

Bishop, A. J. (1990) 'Western mathematics: The secret weapon of cultural imperialism', *Race and Class, 32*(2), 51–65.

Boisselle, L. N. (2016) 'Decolonizing science and science education in a postcolonial space (Trinidad, a Developing Caribbean Nation, illustrates)', *SAGE Open,* 1–11. DOI: 10.1177/2158244016635257

Broadbent, A. (2017) 'African universities must take a critical view of knowledge and how it's made', *The Conversation,* 17 May. Retrieved from https://theconversation.com/african-universities-must-take-a-critical-view-of-knowledge-and-how-its-made-77878

Burnett, D. G. (1999) 'A view from the bridge: The two cultures debate, its legacy, and the history of science', *Daedalus, 128*(2), 193–218.

Castro-Gómez, S. (2002) 'The social sciences, epistemic violence, and the problem of the invention of the other', *Nepantla: Views from South, 3*(2), 269–285.

Cleophas, F. J. (2020) 'Decolonising the South African sport science curriculum', *Sport in Society,* 1–15. DOI: 10.1080/17430437.2020.1752674

Crease, R. P., Martin, J. D. and Staley, R. (2019) 'Decolonizing physics: Learning from the periphery', *Physics in Perspective, 21,* 91–92.

Doran, Y. (2019) *Knowledge building: Developing axiological constellations in Humanities*. Keynote address: Third International LCT Conference. 4 July 2019. Johannesburg. Retrieved 5 August 2021 from www.youtube.com/watch?v=OaAIT0lgSDA

Dube, S. and Banerjee-Dube, I. (Eds.). (2019) *Unbecoming modern: Colonialism, modernity, colonial modernities*. London: Routledge.

Eglash, R. (1997). When math worlds collide: Intention and invention in ethnomathematics. Science, *Technology and Human Values, 22*(1), 79–97.

Eglash, R., Bennett, A., Babbitt, W., Lachney, M., Reinhardt, M. and Hammond-Sowah, D. (2020) 'Decolonizing posthumanism: Indigenous material agency in generative STEM', *British Journal of Educational Technology, 51*(4), 1334–1353.

Glenn, E. L. (2015) *From clashing to matching: Examining the legitimation codes that underpin shifting views about climate change* (Doctoral dissertation). Retrieved 5 August 2021 from https://opus.cloud.lib.uts.edu.au/bitstream/10453/43393/2/02whole.pdf

Green, L. J. (2012) 'Beyond South Africa's indigenous knowledge-science' wars', *South African Journal of Science, 108*(7–8), 44–54.

Gould, S. J. (2000) 'Deconstructing the "science wars" by reconstructing an old mould', *Science, 287*(5451), 253–261.

Hassel, C. A., Tamang, A. L., Foushee, L. and Bull, R. B. H. (2019) 'Decolonizing nutrition science', *Current Developments in Nutrition, 3*(Supplement 2), 3–11.

Henriques, G. (2012) 'Revisiting the science wars – toward a scientific humanistic worldview', *Psychology Today* [Blog post]. Retrieved from www.psychologytoday.com/za/blog/theory-knowledge/201206/revisiting-the-science-wars

Ideland, M. (2018) 'Science, coloniality, and "the great rationality divide"', *Science and Education, 27*(7–8), 783–803.

James, F. A. (2016). Introduction: Some significances of the two cultures debate. *Interdisciplinary Science Reviews, 41*(2–3), 107–117.

Leibowitz, B. (2017) 'Cognitive justice and the higher education curriculum', *Journal of Education (University of KwaZulu-Natal), 68*, 93–112. Retrieved 5 August 2021 from www.scielo.org.za/pdf/jed/n68/06.pdf

Mackerness, E.D. (1960) 'Ignorant armies', *The University Review 33*(1): 14–17

Marker, M. (2019) 'Indigenous STEM success stories as disquieting decolonization: Thoughts on new times and, old thoughts about place-ness', *Cultural Studies of Science Education, 14*(1), 199–204.

Maton, K. (2014a) *Knowledge and knowers: Towards a realist sociology of education*. London: Routledge.

Maton, K. (2014b) 'Building powerful knowledge: The significance of semantic waves'. In B. Barrett and E. Rata (Eds.), *Knowledge and the future of the curriculum* (pp. 181–197). London: Palgrave Macmillan.

Maton, K. and Chen, R.T. (2016) 'LCT in qualitative research: creating a translation device for studying constructivist pedagogy' In K. Maton, S. Hood and S. Shay (Eds.), *Knowledge Building: Educational Studies in Legitimation Code Theory* (pp. 27–s48). London: Routledge

Maton, K. (2020) 'Semantic waves: Context, complexity and academic discourse'. In J. R. Martin, K. Maton and Y. J. Doran (Eds.), *Accessing academic discourse: Systemic functional linguistics and Legitimation Code Theory* (pp. 59–85). London: Routledge.

Maton, K. and Doran, Y. J. (2021) 'Constellating science: How relations among ideas help build knowledge'. In K. Maton, J. R. Martin and Y. J. Doran (Eds.), *Teaching science: Knowledge, language, pedagogy* (pp. 49–75). London: Routledge.

Mazzocchi, F. (2006) 'Western science and traditional knowledge: Despite their variations, different forms of knowledge can learn from each other', *EMBO Reports*, *7*(5), 463–466.

McClintock, A. (2013) *Imperial leather: Race, gender, and sexuality in the colonial contest*. Abingdon: Routledge.

Nicol, C., Gerofsky, S., Nolan, K., Francis, K. and Fritzlan, A. (2020) 'Teacher professional learning with/in place: Storying the work of decolonizing mathematics education from within a colonial structure', *Canadian Journal of Science, Mathematics and Technology Education*, *20*(2), 190–204.

Powers, J. C. (2020) 'The history of Chemistry in chemical education', *Isis*, *111*(3), 576–581.

Rip, A. (2019) 'Recapturing the status of indigenous knowledge and its relation to Western science', *Critical Studies in Teaching and Learning*, *7*(1), 86–107.

Schiebinger, L. L. (2009) *Plants and empire*. Cambridge, MA: Harvard University Press.

Tamarkin, N. (2017) 'Genetic ancestry and decolonizing possibilities', *Catalyst: Feminism, Theory, Technoscience*, *3*(1). Retrieved 5 August 2021 from link.gale. com/apps/doc/A561685917/AONE?u=anon~c12cb811andsid=googleScholarand xid=e4476926.

Tharakan, J. (2017) 'Indigenous knowledge systems for appropriate technology development', *Indigenous People*, 123–134. Retrieved 5 August 2021 from www. intechopen.com/chapters/56259

Vandeyar, S. and Swart, R. (2019) 'Shattering the silence: Dialogic engagement about education protest actions in South African university classrooms', *Teaching in Higher Education*, *24*(6), 772–788.

7 A decolonial science education

How do we move forward?

Margaret A.L. Blackie and Hanelie Adendorff

Introduction

The call for decolonization in the context of science education elicits various responses from academics in the sciences. The first is incredulity followed by a rejection that the idea is even worth discussing. The second is a populist leap into attempts to include local knowledge content without any real critical engagement. The third is a recognition that there may be something to the call for decolonization, but a sense of being overwhelmed by what might actually be required to decolonize in any meaningful way (Costandius *et al.*, 2015). Both the first and second approaches tend to be knee-jerk responses and both are potentially problematic albeit in different ways. In Adendorff and Blackie (2020) we offered an analysis of these positions using the dimensions of Specialization and Autonomy from Legitimation Code Theory (LCT). Helping academic scientists into the third space where it is possible to recognize that there may be merit to engaging with the conversation has been discussed in Chapter 6 of this volume. It is likely that this chapter will be received with confusion by some outside science education as to why such painfully slow steps need to be taken. It may simultaneously be viewed as a profound, paradigm shifting argument from those within the sciences inclined to engage with the conversation. In reading this chapter, we ask you to take cognizance of your own starting point while understanding that our goal is to facilitate the process in science; our intended readers are primarily academic scientists.

The task in this chapter is to examine where we need to begin the journey to decoloniality. In the humanities, the starting point may be the curriculum content itself. We argue here that in the physical or natural sciences the point of departure is not the curriculum content itself but the Western idea of the primacy of the autonomous individual. The invitation for academic scientists is to begin to pay attention to the diversity of human beings sitting

DOI: 10.4324/9781003106968-7

in their lecture theatres rather than the far simpler 'blank slate' upon which scientific understanding is to be imprinted.

Is science socially neutral?

We turn to the work of Maldonado-Torres (2016) who writes about coloniality of power, coloniality of knowledge and coloniality of being.[1] He argues that the modern/colonial conception of knowledge comprises three major elements: subject (and subjectivity), object (and objectivity), and method (and methodology). Whilst there are other ways of conceiving of knowledge, there are no other ways to conceive of *scientific* knowledge. However, situating power, knowledge and being as three interrelated structures which potentially foster and support coloniality gives us an entry into the conversation within science and science education.

We need to begin by acknowledging that legitimate knowledge in science is determined primarily through the manner in which it is produced. There is a direct link between the development of precision instruments in Europe and the establishment of scientific fields. Chemistry only emerged as a scientific field in the nineteenth century with the development of accurate balances which could measure precise masses of substances (Fabbrizzi, 2008). This enabled the development of technology which fueled the first industrial revolution and with this the substantial increase in British colonization. These things are all inextricably linked. Thus, no reimagination of science will decouple the scientific method from the technology of measurement which is strongly associated with Western Europe.

The fact that an experiment performed in a laboratory in Mumbai can be reproduced reliably in Vancouver is taken as fundamental to natural science (Goodman *et al.*, 2016). This reproducibility is an essential part of the scientific method and is a major element of ensuring validity. In these terms, the experiment transcends culture. Provided each scientist is sufficiently trained in the skills required to both carry out the experiment and to analyze the data produced there should be no difference in the outcome of the experiment, regardless of where it is performed. To this end, science can be seen as being 'objective' in the sense that the cultural background of the person performing the experiment is irrelevant.

Yet, more recent scrutiny has shown that this concept of reproducibility can be less reliable in particular instances than the ideal would suggest (Goodman *et al.*, 2016). Furthermore, the meaning of reproducibility varies across the natural and physical sciences. Nonetheless, it is upon this concept that the 'objectivity' of science rests. However, it is clear from the work of Kuhn (1977) that there is a distinct difference between the objectivity in the consensus position of the scientific field and the position held by an individual scientist. The individual scientist is profoundly influenced by the mental paradigm into which they were inducted. Boas' notion of sound blindness is a useful illustration. Sound blindness is the term used to describe the observation of anthropologists describing sounds made in foreign languages. These anthropologists were substantially influenced by their own native tongue (Boas, 1889; Roepstorff *et al.*, 2010). They could not hear some variations in speech in foreign languages precisely because they had been conditioned to hear the particular variations inherent to their mother-tongue. Scientists are similarly shaped by the paradigm of theory through which they intellectually entered the field (Kuhn, 2012). Thus, we must be careful not to uncritically confer the objectivity of science upon any individual scientist (McComas, 1996).

The subjectivity indicated by both Boas and Kuhn is complemented by the recognition that when one begins to explore the history of any particular science it is clear that the experience of the scientist plays more of a role in determining what should be explored and what counts as legitimate knowledge than the current rhetoric of the objectivity of science allows. A simple example of this was the variety of experiments performed to ascertain the age of the Earth. The current measure the age of the Earth was determined using the half-life of radioactive elements (Burchfield, 1975). The internal consistency between different combinations of isotopes means that the answer is fairly well determined. Yet, at the turn of the twentieth century radioactivity itself was barely known and the discovery of the neutron which accounts for the isotopes was still decades away. The problem had presented itself through Darwin's *Origin of the Species* (1859) and Lyell's *Principles of Geology* (1853). It was clear that 'deep time' was necessary to explain both the biological variation and the geological stratification which was so evident. Several scientists stepped up to find an answer this question. Two examples serve to illustrate the point. Kelvin, knowledgeable in thermodynamics, calculated the age of the Earth to be between 20 and 100 million years old. He used the heat transfer between the Sun and the Earth, and transfer within the Earth itself. Alas, the absence of knowledge of plate tectonics, nuclear fusion and radioactivity meant his calculations were fatally flawed (Burchfield, 1975). Joly likewise turned to a subject he knew about. He used the concentration of sodium in sea water to offer an estimate of 80–100 million years (Joly, 1900), the logic being that the sodium had come from rocks through erosion and had thus increased in concentration over time. Again, some of his assumptions turned out to be false (Macdougall, 2009).

The point here is that a major question had arisen from new scientific data and these scientists tried to solve the problem using the intellectual resources at their disposal. The methods they used were well-known and both Kelvin and Joly would probably have been capable of reproducing the procedure presented by the other, but the creation of a possible solution was individual to each scientist. Joly would not have used thermodynamics and Kelvin would not have used sodium concentration. It is at this level that science is deeply influenced by the experience of the individual scientist and, thus, both subjective and highly creative (McComas, 1996). The scientist will approach a problem with their personal lexicon. The verification of their experiments by the scientific community then pulls the data generated and the conclusions drawn into greater objectivity (Kuhn, 1977).

Using the epistemic plane to describe scientific training

Our purpose in this chapter is to examine scientific training so that we can uncover what decolonization may look like in the natural sciences. Drawing on the Specialization dimension from Legitimation Code Theory (Maton, 2014), science and science education may be considered as being a claim about something (*epistemic relations*) and made by someone (*social relations*). We discuss this in detail later in this chapter. At this point we shall explore *epistemic relations* in more detail. Against the backdrop of the example of Kelvin and Joly trying to solve the problem of the age of the Earth, we turn more broadly to the training of scientists using the *epistemic plane*, as shown in Figure 7.1. Epistemic relations refer to practices which may vary both in what they relate to (*ontic relations*) and in how they relate (*discursive relations*).[2] Both ontic relations and discursive relations can vary in strengths along a continuum. Bringing those two strengths together gives what are termed in LCT, *insights* (Maton, 2014). There are an infinite number of possible strengths, but LCT also identifies four key insights, as shown in Figure 7.1.

Situational insights can be understood as procedural pluralism, meaning there is more than one acceptable way to solve a problem. Practices expound strong boundaries around legitimate objects of study but weaker boundaries around which approaches one can legitimately take to address those objects (Maton, 2014). That is, the problem is clearly defined but multiple solutions could be acceptable. This is illustrated in the different approaches taken by Joly and Kelvin described earlier to solve the same problem.

Purist insights strongly bound both legitimate objects of study and legitimate ways in which the study is carried out (Maton, 2014). For example, a PhD project in chemistry will require a well defined object of study recognized to be a chemical problem, will require the use of methods which are recognized as valid to solve this particular problem and will need to be described in a manner consistent with established literary conventions of chemistry.

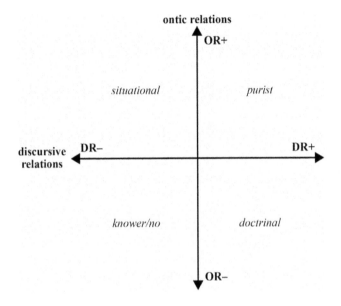

Figure 7.1 The epistemic plane (Maton, 2014, p. 177)

Doctrinal insights can be understood as methodological dogmatism, meaning only specific, well defined methods are acceptable as legitimate. The approach used is strongly bounded but legitimate objects of study are relatively weakly bounded (Maton, 2014). Here one is demonstrating mastery of a method but any object to which that method may legitimately be applied is acceptable. The focus in scientific training can be narrowly constrained to mastery of the method (stronger discursive relations) whilst omitting details of the constraints of application (downplaying ontic relations). Thus, one can master the method but not necessarily understand how it may be applied to other problems (Engelbrecht *et al.*, 2005; Potgieter and Davidowitz, 2011). This tends to be the level of most of science education at an undergraduate level in South Africa. The student has sufficient pattern recognition that they can go through the steps of 'solving' a problem presented in a familiar format. However, they may have no real grasp of the underlying principles, or indeed, any sense of the limitations of the method. In terms of the age of the Earth example described earlier, when it is taught, radioactive decay will be presented as the gold standard of determination of age. No other method would be deemed acceptable. However, this method is only applicable to things which are not living. To extend the example, a student, seeing the application of the method using radioactive carbon to the

Shroud of Turin (made from cotton cloth where the radioactive carbon content is fixed), may try to apply it to aging of the Giant Redwoods which are older. However, the trees are still living and carbon is being exchanged with the environment, therefore the radioactive carbon content is being continually refreshed. This means the method could be faithfully applied but the answer generated by the data will be inherently erroneous.

Knower/no insights occur when neither legitimate methods of inquiry nor legitimate objects of study are constrained (Maton, 2014). In science this insight can be employed when a new field is emerging – such as the field of inquiry which arose out of the question of the age of Earth. Initially, the object of the study and the methods used were entirely open. Kelvin's object of inquiry was the temperature of the Earth using methods from thermodynamics, and Joly's object was the concentration of salt in sea water using methods from solubility studies. The object of study in an emerging field requires both a weakening of the boundaries around what can legitimately be studied and a weakening of boundaries around the manner in which the study should be carried out. As the field matures it is likely that ontic relations and/or discursive relations will strengthen.

Drawing from the context of teaching organic chemistry at a tertiary institution one way of understanding science education can be as movement around this plane. Novice students begin in the knower/no insight. At the beginning of their study, they have little sense of the bounds of a particular subject or of the manner in which knowledge is or can be constructed. The journey begins by learning some of the procedures which are acceptable thereby entering a doctrinal insight, but they may be unaware of the constraints of application of those procedures (DR is strengthening but OR is not yet visible to the student). As time goes by, they learn some of the ways in which the knowledge field is carved into sub-fields and herein purist insights begin to emerge (OR becomes visible and begins to strengthen). And finally, they are presented with a problem which they must be able to identify within a specific knowledge area (OR is strengthening) and then solve though applying diverse methods (DR is beginning to weaken), thus moving towards a situational insight. As discursive relations weaken, so the use of individual creativity may increase.

In the example of the age of the Earth problem it can be argued that both Lord Kelvin and Professor Joly began with a *purist insight*. That is, they were both experts in using a particular set of well defined procedures (DR+) to solve problems within a well defined knowledge area (OR+). The new problem pushed them into a *situational insight* where a plurality of methods could be applied to a clearly defined problem (weakening discursive relations). In engaging with the problem, it became clear that the assumptions which both had to make to apply the procedure faithfully meant that they were moving out of their clearly bounded field (weakening ontic relations). Hence, they were tipped inadvertently into a *knower/no insight*. At this point, both Joly and Kelvin made errors based on their assumptions. Nonetheless, both men were in a position to state the assumptions that they had made because they had already been trained in a way which made recognizing the limits of their experiments clear.

The trained scientist may embark on an entirely new field of study which requires the development of novel methodologies. Nonetheless, the training they would have been through will profoundly influence their manner of engagement with the new field. In other words, there is a degree of personal formation that happens in the process of training the scientist. Thus, becoming a scientist is not just about the appropriation of knowledge (epistemic relations), it also impacts one's way of being in the world (social relations). We will now turn to the *specialization plane* from LCT to explore the interplay between epistemic relations and social relations.

Why is the human person overlooked in science education?

Specialization from LCT allows us to see that what it is to be 'educated' in different knowledge areas is substantially divergent for good reasons. Specialization distinguishes between epistemic relations (ER) and social relations (SR) (Figure 7.2) (Maton, 2014).

In the natural sciences, specialized knowledge, procedures and skills are often emphasized as the basis of knowledge claims (relatively strong epistemic relations, ER+) – and one's personal and social attributes are downplayed as the basis of knowledge claims (relatively weak social relations, SR−). Thus, the natural sciences tend to typically (though not always) represent different forms of a 'knowledge code'. The reverse tends (but again not always) to be true in many humanities subjects: specialized knowledge, procedures and skills are relatively downplayed (ER−) and personal attributes are emphasized (SR+) – a 'knower code'. It is important to note that there is no one 'ideal' form of any of the codes represented on the plane (Figure 7.2) as there is infinite variation of epistemic relations and social relations both across and within disciplines.

Returning to the primary consideration of this chapter – science education and decoloniality – we find a 'code clash' occurring. A 'code clash' occurs when practices exhibit different bases of legitimacy (Maton, 2014). Decolonial arguments, typically situated in a knower code, are used to critique science. Importantly this code clash is also responsible for the inability of many academic scientists to see the relevance of decolonization to science and science education (Adendorff and Blackie, 2020).

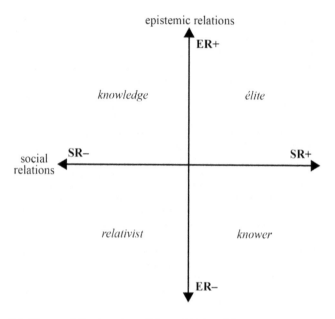

Figure 7.2 The specialization plane (Maton, 2014, p. 30)

The scientists offering the argument of the impossibility of science being colonizing because it is 'objective' are 'knower-blind'. Whilst the students demanding Newton's Laws be dropped are 'knowledge-blind'. The terms knower-blind and knowledge-blind are discussed in detail later. However, all social practices have both epistemic relations and social relations in operation regardless of what is valorized in the particular field. Put another way, decoloniality is both a knowledge problem and a knower problem but one has to begin with the structure of the field itself to determine the most appropriate starting point.

Knowledge-blindness

Our task here is not to revisit the entire argument for the existence of knowledge-blindness, but simply to reflect on the key points, so that by contrast we can show that knower-blindness may be as significant in the natural sciences.

In *Knowledge and Knowers*, Maton writes:

> Never has knowledge been viewed as so crucial to the nature of society. Yet, *understanding knowledge* is not viewed as crucial to *understanding*

society. For what unites accounts of social change is not only their emphasis on the centrality of knowledge but also their lack of a theory of knowledge. Knowledge is described as a defining feature of modern societies, but what that knowledge is, its form and its effects, are not part of the analysis.

(Maton, 2014, p. 1, original emphases)

This critique is primarily aimed at sociological approaches to education research. As Alexander argued, much education literature is mired in an 'epistemological dilemma' created by a false dichotomy between positivist absolutism and constructivist relativism (Alexander, 1995). That is, knowledge is either understood as 'decontextualised, value-free, detached and certain or as socially constructed within cultural and historical conditions in ways that reflect vested social interests' (Maton, 2014, p. 2).

As the twentieth century proceeded it became increasingly clear in some fields in the humanities and social sciences that one's social position had a significant impact on how one engaged with information and constructed knowledge. Positivist absolutism was anathema and in this false dichotomy the only other option was to follow constructivist relativism, which holds that there is nothing real beyond the mental construction (Alexander, 1995). In this paradigm, everyone is a valid knower. Knowledge itself disappears from view and power relations become all important. The mark of being 'educated' is no longer what one knows but 'knowing' in the way that is deemed to be acceptable by those in power in education.

Specialization offers us a path out of this impasse. The false dichotomy is replaced by two orthogonal, and therefore independent, variables. In revealing the dynamic interplay between epistemic relations and social relations both the knowledge and the knower in any field come into view. In a knower-code field, the detail of what is taught is de-emphasized and teaching the student how to interact with the information in such a way as to be seen as a legitimate knower is emphasized, described as developing the appropriate gaze (Maton, 2014). Here choosing texts and authors which speak more directly to the experience of the students may be a reasonable quest. Indeed, the recognition of the ways in which Western modernity has profoundly shaped the very way in which study of the humanities and social sciences is conducted is necessarily a part of the decolonial conversation (Heleta, 2016). Nonetheless, our quest for an education that is appropriate for twenty-first-century South Africa cannot eliminate the impact of Western civilization (Mbembe, 2016). Rather we need to look at the elements which are simply taken for granted in Western modernity. One example is the Western presumption of the primacy of the individual versus the African cultural concept of ubuntu.

In a knower code then, we must examine what is taught. The development of a truly decolonial curriculum is likely to require changing the texts and sources used. It will also require an iterative method to critique the use of concepts and scaffold ideas which are themselves bound to Western civilization. Whilst the former can be achieved relatively quickly, the latter will take years as academics themselves begin to find new ways of exploring and expressing these knowledge areas (Mbembe, 2016). Indeed, the task of decolonial education in a knower code is fundamentally about the development of culturally embedded knowledge practices.

The challenge is a little different in a knowledge code. To substitute Western scientific knowledge with indigenous knowledge is not the place to begin. This approach would substantially erode the value of scientific education. To change the foundation would be to erase scientific knowledge and begin from scratch. Again we must acknowledge here that the modern/colonial conception of knowledge (Maldonado-Torres, 2016) is congruent with, and indistinguishable from, the scientific conception of knowledge.

To present indigenous knowledge systems as science is problematic. This is not because the knowledge itself is suspect; indeed there may be a great deal of very useful information held in these systems. However, what makes scientific knowledge 'scientific' is the method used to verify claims to knowledge, as it is upon the basis of the method that the knowledge claim is made. In order to bring in traditional knowledge systems we have to ask about the manner in which this knowledge has come to be known. If one considers acupuncture as a traditional knowledge system, the knowledge held in the system is powerful and can provide a viable method of healing. However, the language used to communicate what is happening is descriptive, rather than explanatory. Thus whilst the knowledge within acupuncture can be used to good effect it does not have a scientific basis. This does not make acupuncture inherently less valuable; it just means that its inclusion in a science curriculum may create confusion. However, ultimately we will need to find a way to work with different knowledge systems in our education system. That is to say, we need to be very careful about blurring the lines too quickly. It is not our purpose in this chapter to make any move towards disrupting the boundaries of science education. That may well be necessary in time but there is preparation to be done first.

As we have argued elsewhere, we have to find a way of examining what is at stake in science education (Adendorff and Blackie, 2020). Is there a need to decolonize the project of science education even within the narrow confines of its current conception? We argue here that there is such a need. There are doubtless many routes towards a decolonial science curriculum, and we are not claiming that we have arrived, but one has to begin somewhere. Our proposition is that where the knower code fields may have been knowledge-blind, there may be an equivalent 'knower-blindness' in knowledge code fields. Thus our starting point is to argue for the importance of making the knower visible in science and in science education. This focus on knower-blindness opens the door to making visible the coloniality of power and coloniality of being (Maldonado-Torres, 2016), which are unconsciously operational in science.

Knower-blindness

Let us return to the false dichotomy where knowledge is either understood as 'decontextualised, value-free, detached and certain or as socially constructed within cultural and historical conditions in ways that reflect vested social interests' (Maton, 2014, p. 2). In the light of this erroneous juxtaposition it is no wonder that many scientists simply dismiss any calls for decoloniality. Many natural scientists will stand firmly in the value-free zone and presume their educative efforts will follow suit. In fairness, we should perhaps add a little nuance. Most scientists would happily accept decontextualized, value-free and detached knowledge, but would not agree to absolute certainty. We know that what we teach is the best current version of our understanding; many scientists would replace certainty with reliability.

The real power of scientific knowledge is that it is transferable across cultures. Newton's Laws accurately predict the movement of large objects regardless of whether the interaction is observed in Greenland or Argentina. The social standing, political leaning or religious affiliation of the person carrying out the scientific experiment is irrelevant. Whilst scientific knowledge is entirely transferable and acultural, neither the scientific project nor science education is in fact socially neutral. The person of the scientist, shaped by their life experience, will deeply impact their approach to their own projects and their approach to education (Aikenhead, 1996). It is at this level, then, that the project of decoloniality can begin.

Decoloniality in science education

We have found that it is more helpful to approach decoloniality in our context from an experiential point of view rather than a theoretical one (see Chapter 6, this volume). The reason for this is that many academic scientists have very little basic epistemology.[3] Few have had much exposure to knowledge creation that is not rooted in the scientific method and bound to physical measurement. Thus, they can tend to lack respect for academic research generated outside a positivist or realist paradigm. So, we have found it more productive to use illustrations and personal experience to enable academic scientists to begin to see the importance of the conversation. To this end, we have found that it is much easier for academic scientists to recognize that some students in their classes may experience a sense of not belonging and/ or a cultural barrier. One source of such negative experience is the use of real world illustrations which may be beyond the experience of those from a different culture and/or social class.

An example of this could be to illustrate increasing rotational velocity using the change in speed that occurs when an ice skater pulls in their arms during a spin. The image of the ice skater may work well in Europe or North America where ice-skating is a fairly regular winter time activity. In sub-Saharan Africa, only reasonably well-off city dwelling children would have had any experience of going to an ice-rink. The middle-class students may be able to make the imaginative leap or have the social confidence to know that the incapacity to make the mental leap is not essential to the topic in hand. A student from a more rural, working-class setting, in struggling to understand the illustration, may not immediately recognize that it is not important to the concept. More significantly, if the student feels out of their depth socially, they are far less likely to admit the lack of understanding. The net result is alienation: a feeling of not belonging experienced because the lecturer, in an attempt to make a concept more accessible, inadvertently used an illustration without considering whether it was actually experientially accessible to everyone in the class.

The simplest start towards decoloniality is an awareness that even though the concepts we teach do not immediately appear to be culturally bound, we do nonetheless teach in and through a cultural paradigm. In the natural sciences, we tend to be blind to social and cultural influence precisely because of the insistence on the objectivity of science. To be a scientist is partly to actively forget that I have been formed in a particular culture as soon as I enter the laboratory, and this mentality gets transferred to lecture theaters. Knower-blindness is not just an accident of the system, it is actively endorsed.

Once the academic scientist has begun to recognize that we bring cultural baggage into our lecture theatres and laboratories, a major source of resistance to the concept of decoloniality has been overcome. The acknowledgement of the cultural baggage brings the coloniality of power into view (Maldonado-Torres, 2016). Here the scientist may begin to recognize that their way of being in the world will impact their interaction with their students. This is the equivalent of Boas recognizing that sound blindness is a real phenomenon. This is an important and necessary first step, but in itself is insufficient for the overall project.

The second, deeper level requires a recognition that social relations do require some attention in science education. This level will ultimately call forth the recognition of the coloniality of being (Maldonado-Torres, 2016) but will require deep engagement to develop new ways of being. Once again, the project of forming scientists is typically located in a knowledge code (relatively strong epistemic relations and relatively weak social relations). Note though, 'relatively weak' social relations do not mean that these relations are absent. The question, then, is how we develop a model of science education that takes into account the human person without eroding the strength of epistemic relations. Here we need to remember the power of Specialization, which allows for independent variation of epistemic relations and social relations in direct contrast to the false dichotomy, which would require sacrificing the power of science knowledge to the service of enculturation (see earlier sections). That is to say we can strengthen social relations without necessarily eroding epistemic relations.

We turn now to the work of Lonergan. We acknowledge that some may well reject using the work of yet another dead white man to help towards the project of decoloniality, but he provides a model which allows us to bring the social relations into view whilst holding true to the essence of robust conceptual understanding which underpins the stronger epistemic relations of the sciences.

Lonergan

Lonergan's project was to understand what it means to understand (Lonergan, 1992). In his method he drew on mathematics, common sense and other divergent knowledge areas precisely because he wanted an explanation that could cover any experience which we would recognize as understanding. Lonergan's desire was to make visible to process of understanding such that it would help any person become a more conscious, reflective and engaged adult, regardless of their chosen sphere.

It is important recognize that the canon of science, which includes reproducibility and cross-cultural transfer, does come with a universalizing claim to 'truth'. Although 'truth' must be understood to mean that which the community has deemed to be the best description of reality we have yet to produce, this may feel hegemonic and brutish to those who work within some knower codes. Nonetheless, we hope that it will be received with a generosity of spirit which will be able to recognize the essence we must preserve if science is to retain its inherent strength and trustworthiness.

Further to the scientific claim to 'truth' being underpinned by the recognition that our current theories are the best yet, new data may arise that will require rethinking and a Kuhnian paradigm shift (Kuhn, 2012). Not all scientific knowledge is of equal rigour and some theories underpin a far larger range of experimental findings than others. We are unlikely to completely rethink evolution or atomic theory, but some of the assumptions that have been made have indeed been reconfigured over time in the light of new discoveries.

The point of making this explicit here is to say that within science there is an established and accepted canon of the necessary foundations of the scientific disciplines. For example, it would be highly peculiar to find an undergraduate chemistry curriculum that failed to cover the Periodic Table or a biology curriculum that failed to cover the classification of organisms. This is precisely what is meant by having stronger epistemic relations. The 'what' that is 'known' matters. Thus, the model of education and decoloniality we employ in our own contexts must take this into account. Once again, it is not at clear at this point in time that one can decouple science from the coloniality of knowledge (Maldonado-Torres, 2016).

Lonergan's model of understanding gives us four steps (Lonergan, 1992). His goal is not simply for me to understand but for me to know that I understand. To achieve this I will need:

> *Experience*, which comprises the learning experience including lectures, tutorials, textbooks, etc., and any prior experience which will influence the way in which I interact with my learning environment. The latter will include cultural considerations, language, and any prior learning.
>
> *Insight*, which is the beautiful 'aha' moment where the fragments of experience click into place and something is understood.
>
> *Judgement*, which requires reflection. Is my insight correct? That is, is my insight in line with that which I am being taught? It is at this point where we must insist in science that there is 'correct understanding' and that correct understanding means in line with current understanding held by the scientific community, rather than claiming an absolute truth.
>
> *Decision making*, which is based on my judgement of whether my understanding is correct, partially correct or incorrect, leading to some action being required. The decision making step is taken to ascertain the appropriate action.

The first step, *experience*, requires engagement with community – as humans we learn from one another and our experience is framed by prior learning. Even if no other person is physically present, a textbook is still written by another human being. The second step, *insight*, is individual. The moment of insight is interior to the mind of one person, even if this happens in the presence of another who has helped place the pieces so that they can cohere. The third step, *judgement*, will again require engagement with the community. It is impossible to ascertain correct understanding without checking what the community understands. Again, this may simply be re-reading a paragraph in a text book but it is still a communal activity. Finally, *decision making* is individual but it will have a communal effect. My decisions will impact my world in some way.

In the context of science education then we can do very little about the structure of the knowledge itself. Nonetheless, the conscious engagement with others to verify the knowledge begins to make visible both 'being' and 'power'. Many academic scientists, ourselves included, have happily sent students on their way once they get to that beautiful aha moment, presuming that they have understood correctly simply because something has 'clicked'. We fail to ask the students what they think they understand. We take the experience of insight at face value and presume that it is correct understanding. However just because there is some experience of connection and sense making does not mean that there is correct understanding (Lonergan, 1992). The scientific project itself is never a lone activity regardless of the caricature of the mad professor or the individualist way in which the scientific method is sometimes presented (McComas, 1996). The judgement and decision making parts of the process are an inherent part of the scientific method and require engagement with the community. The fact that we fail to make that explicit to students is a significant failure in the educational project. This engagement with the community will impact the way in which the student understands their position in the world and therefore will certainly impact their being, and in time will have an influence on how power is distributed.

In terms of the decolonial project, we argued in the opening section of this chapter that one area of Western modernity which is highly problematic is the primacy of the notion of the autonomous individual. The vagaries of individual preferences are to be followed without any cognizance of impact on the community. Lonergan's model immediately highlights two important areas where culture and community can be directly engaged. The first is in the simple recognition of the significance of the diversity of lived experiences within the student cohort. As described earlier, any real life examples must be examples which are truly accessible to all students or the students should be asked to offer their own examples which illustrate the concept. We have found that is a powerful aid to conceptual gain in itself as examples are then shared – this widens the repertoire of the lecturer and all the students. Furthermore, misconceptions can be revealed as poor examples emerge and afford a useful teaching opportunity. At a deeper level, there can be a real validation of the diversity of experience, which helps mitigate alienation. Importantly, this process is also illuminating for the lecturer.

They learn a good deal about the students sitting in front of them. This personal interaction ultimately has the potential to shift everyone in the lecture theatre a little (or a lot).

Second, the recognition that both judgement and decision making are activities which require engagement with community shifts the educative paradigm. This is no longer pouring knowledge into an empty vessel to create a 'mini-me'. It is a deeply empowering experience which will shape the way the student (and ultimately the scientist) engages with the world. We are no longer teaching science then to fill the 'science' bucket in the brain, what we are actually doing is formative. Importantly, the emphasis on communal engagement means that we are immediately diverging from one of the most toxic and problematic aspects of Western modernity – the primacy of the idea of the autonomous individual where my individual 'freedom' trumps any social responsibility. If science education is focused only on conceptual understanding, we will continue, unconsciously and blindly, to foster this mindset. Shifting to the recognition that engagement with the scientific community is an indispensable part of the process makes the myth of the autonomous individual much harder to sustain.

Conclusion

The project of decoloniality within the natural sciences is substantially different from that in other knowledge areas. The main reason for this is the inextricable link between a colonial construction of knowledge and science. However, there is real space to reveal the coloniality of power and coloniality of being to which science is almost entirely blind. This chapter is written primarily for scientists using the tools of social science to show that we have a credible starting point. In this chapter we do not claim to have clarity on what decolonial science education will look like. It will take a substantial culture shift within natural science itself to achieve that. What we propose here is an entry point.

We have argued that one major issue which needs to be addressed in the decolonial project in science results from the 'knower-blindness' and the concept of the autonomous individual. Knower-blindness results in a conflation of the objectivity of science and the objectivity of the scientist, which hitherto has been at the heart of Western modernity. This means that the scientist is presumed to be acting objectively and so any critiques of the uses of science are easily fobbed off. Decolonial science education means that we pay attention to this conflation by introducing an awareness of the variation of experience in the student body, which necessarily shifts the non-reflexive tendency to universalize the experience of the lecturer.

The primacy of the individual results in the perpetuation of the valorization of the rights of the individual over any consideration of what it is best for society. Here embedding a process of reflection in a model which requires us to pay attention to the presence of the scientific community is at least an entry into eroding the lack of awareness of the significance of others. We hope we have shown that through the dual lens of Legitimation Code Theory and Lonergan's model of understanding, there is a way to take cognizance of the importance of the human person in their context and facilitate scientific dialogue in such a way that society itself can be transformed in a way that does not inherently erode the knowledge which must be the basis of any credible science education.

Notes

1 The distinction between coloniality and colonization is discussed at length in Chapter 4 of this volume. The distinction is not central to the argument in this chapter.
2 The relationship of the *epistemic plane* to the Specialization dimension of LCT is discussed in Chapter 6 of this volume.
3 This is perhaps cause to take seriously the concept of pluriversalism discussed in Chapter 5 of this volume.

References

Adendorff, H. and Blackie, M. A. (2020) 'Decolonizing the science curriculum: When good intentions are not enough'. In C. Winberg, S. McKenna and K. Wilmot (Eds.), *Building knowledge in higher education: Enhancing teaching and learning with Legitimation Code Theory* (pp. 237–254). London: Routledge.

Aikenhead, G. S. (1996) 'Science education: Border crossing into the subculture of science', *Studies in Science Education, 27*(1), 1–52.

Alexander, J. C. (1995) *Fin de siècle social theory: Relativism, reduction, and the problem of reason.* London: Verso.

Boas, F. (1889) 'On alternating sounds', *American Anthropologist, 2*(1), 47–54.

Burchfield, J. D. (1975) 'Radioactivity and the age of the Earth'. In *Lord Kelvin and the age of the earth* (pp. 163–211). London: Macmillan Education UK.

Costandius, E., Blackie, M., Leibowitz, B., Nell, I., Malgas, R., Rosochacki, S. O. and Young, G. (2015) 'Stumbling over the first hurdle? Exploring notions of critical citizenship'. In M. Davies and R. Barnett (Eds.), *The Palgrave handbook of critical thinking in higher education* (pp. 545–558). New York: Palgrave Macmillan US.

Darwin, C. (1859) *On the origin of species by means of natural selection or the preservation of favoured races in the struggle for life.* London: International Book Company.

Engelbrecht, J., Harding, A. and Potgieter, M. (2005) 'Undergraduate students' performance and confidence in procedural and conceptual mathematics', *International Journal of Mathematical Education in Science and Technology, 36*(7), 701–712.

Fabbrizzi, L. (2008) 'Communicating about matter with symbols: Evolving from alchemy to chemistry', *Journal of Chemical Education*, *85*(10), 1501–1511.

Goodman, S. N., Fanelli, D. and Ioannidis, J. P. A. (2016) 'What does research reproducibility mean?', *Science Translational Medicine*, *8*(341), 1–12.

Heleta, S. (2016) 'Decolonisation of higher education: Dismantling epistemic violence and Eurocentrism in South Africa', *Transformation in Higher Education*, *1*(1), 1–8.

Joly, J. (1900) 'IV – The geological age of the earth', *Geological Magazine*, *7*(5), 220–225.

Kuhn, T. S. (1977 [2003]) 'Objectivity, value judgment, and theory choice'. In A. Bird and J. Ladyman (Eds.), *Arguing about science* (pp. 74–86). London: Routledge.

Kuhn, T. S. (2012) *The structure of scientific revolutions*. Chicago, IL: University of Chicago Press.

Lonergan, B. (1992) *Insight: A study of human understanding*. Vol. 3. Toronto: University of Toronto Press.

Lyell, C. (1853) *Principles of geology: Or the modern changes of the earth and its inhabitants considered as illustrative of geology*. London: John Murray Publishers.

Macdougall, J. D. (2009) *Nature's clocks: How scientists measure the age of almost everything*. Berkeley: University of California Press.

Maldonado-Torres, N. (2016) *Outline of ten theses on coloniality and decoloniality*. Frantz Fanon Foundation.

Maton, K. (2014) *Knowledge and knowers: Towards a realist sociology of education*. London: Routledge.

Mbembe, A. J. (2016) 'Decolonizing the university: New directions', *Arts and Humanities in Higher Education*, *15*(1), 29–45.

McComas, W. F. (1996) 'Ten myths of science: Reexamining what we think we know about the nature of science', *School Science and Mathematics*, *96*(1), 10–16.

Potgieter, M. and Davidowitz, B. (2011) 'Preparedness for tertiary chemistry: Multiple applications of the Chemistry Competence Test for diagnostic and prediction purposes', *Chemistry Education Research and Practice*, *12*(2), 193–204.

Roepstorff, A., Niewöhner, J. and Beck, S. (2010) 'Enculturing brains through patterned practices', *Neural Networks*, *23*(8–9), 1051–1059.

Name index

Subject index

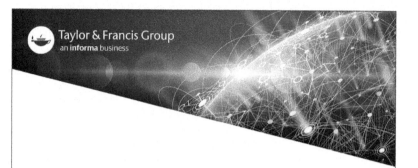